Ge

D0322859

University of the
West of England

BRISTOL

**ST. MATTHIAS
LIBRARY**

This book should be returned by the last date
stamped below.

Georges Bataille

Core Cultural Theorist

Paul Hegarty

SAGE Publications Ltd
6 Bonhill Street
London EC2A 4PU

SAGE Publications Inc
2455 Teller Road
Thousand Oaks, California 91320

SAGE Publications India Pvt Ltd
32, M-Block Market
Greater Kailash – I
New Delhi 110 048

British Library Cataloguing in Publication data

A catalogue record for this book is
available from the British Library

ISBN 0 7619 6077 5
ISBN 0 7619 6078 3 (pbk)

Library of Congress catalog card number 00 133432

Typeset by M Rules
Printed in Great Britain by Biddles Ltd,
Guildford, Surrey

Contents

Note on References

In the main body of the book, all texts are referred to by their title, or by a shortened title when appropriate. Further details are to be found in the bibliography. All texts by Bataille are referred to by their English title, and every reference is accompanied by its location in Bataille's complete works (*Œuvres complètes* [*OC*]). In order to facilitate cross-referencing, full details of all works (in French and in English) by Bataille that are cited in this book can be consulted in the bibliography. Where there is an existing translation, it is referred to. If not, the translations, of titles and of quotations, are my own.

Acknowledgements

Thanks of course to family, friends and colleagues. Particular thanks go to Graham Allen, Ben Andrews, Larry Brown, Anne Frémiot, Martin Halliwell, Colin Harrison, Mike Hawkins, Michael Hoar, Fiona Kearney, Neil Leach, Dave Murray, Keith Reader, Jean-Xavier Ridon, Jon Simons, Judith Still, Clare Whatling, Matt Whitman. I would also like to acknowledge the work of those who have already worked extensively on Bataille, and to whom I have not really had space to do justice, in the text: Julian Pefanis, Michèle Richman, Denis Hollier, Michael Richardson, Georges Didi-Huberman, Nick Land, Francis Marmande.

Introduction

Georges Bataille is, along with Jean-Paul Sartre, Simone de Beauvoir and Michel Foucault, one of the central figures in twentieth-century French thought. At various stages in this century, a particular figure has come to dominate French thought, has been a *maître à penser* (master thinker), with Sartre the archetypal version of this, but it would be excessive to think of Bataille in these terms – in his lifetime he was more of a shadowy presence, known to many within philosophy or aesthetics, but not known on a wider scale. Besides, even Beauvoir was in the shadow of Sartre's pre-eminence. Bataille's writings have taken on a greater significance since his death in 1962, as it has gradually become clear just how influential he has been on the major writers of today.

Bataille's appearance through the texts of others is more than a question of simple influence, even if many, including Jacques Derrida, Michel Foucault, Julia Kristeva and Jean Baudrillard, are heavily indebted to their reading of Bataille. The renown of these writers has led to the reappraisal of those (such as Bataille) referred to in their texts, and in fact, the reading enacted by such writers has also proved to be a *writing* of Bataille – introducing him, and making him a precursor.

In addition to this overt process of influence, Bataille's writing seems in tune with contemporary theories (post-structuralism, various of the postmodernisms around), such that he can be regarded ... perhaps, despite himself,

'perfected future' is in a position to judge. The example of Bataille is in fact a striking confirmation of the claim made by the generation of writers referred to above, to the effect that there can be nothing inherent in a piece of writing, and nothing that faithfully represents its author. The author exists in 'his' absence: the absence that is the written word; the literal absence of death (and posterity); the absence of the author's 'own view' that traditional criticism values so much it has to create it.

As a result, we find we are in more of a circular relation to the writer in question (as we always have to be aware of the retro-spective judgement, retrospective influence on a writer's importance), and if we take this for granted, we will save ourselves much of the ridiculous activity of 'finding' the true, definitive sources for a writer's texts. In practical terms, this means that we do not forget that Bataille read and wrote on Hegel, Marcel Mauss or Nietzsche, but we do refuse to make these into determining instances on the 'thought of Bataille', because for us who come after, the text of Bataille is just as much 'influenced' by later writers such as Derrida or Foucault. As we will see later, Bataille (via Mauss and Derrida) has such a point to make himself – an approach that aims to make us rethink indebtedness, such that it does not correspond to 'owing everything to', but to an open process of gift, receipt and debt.

If we cannot have 'the author', and find his true intentions and sources, can we find the 'man behind the work'? Yes, but this 'man', emerging from behind the 'façade' of the work, is itself only a con-struct. Nowhere does it seem more the case that the 'man behind the work' is to be constructed from the writing than with Bataille. Michel Surya's would-be definitive biography, *Georges Bataille: la mort à l'œuvre*, has almost nothing to say that does not emanate directly from the writings of Bataille.[2] The writer, as the 'man', is only important as an effect of the *œuvre*, and this work has itself to be (re)constructed – a process that starts for Bataille in the special edition of *Critique* of 1963 (*Critique 195–196: Hommage à Georges Bataille*), shortly after his death. Only in the absence of the man does the work come out, and only in the presence of the work is the absence of the writer noted, such that the work becomes the absence of the present writer (in this case, there is the very literal example of Bataille's pornographic novels losing, in the course of the 1960s, the anonymous authorship they had up until then retained). The *œuvre* can only emerge from a sense of completion (even though Bataille's writing resists closure as completion), and in general, writers have had to wait much longer than he did for the recognition of an edition of *Œuvres complètes*. The first volume came out in 1970, only eight years after his death, and the series was completed in 1988.

In this introduction, I propose to keep biographical details to a minimum, regarding them as products rather than sources of the *œuvre*. If the 'man' Georges Bataille is to be minimized, if not effectively denied, then what is 'Georges Bataille'? This too is a construct of writing – Georges Bataille exists at a distance, through his writing, and through his writing only. Any 'I' that was possessed by a real Georges Bataille is of no relevance, taking its meaning only (ever) from the naming, from the becoming 'I'. Whilst it would be a caricature of structuralism to say that this means he is just a 'textual effect' (which is not to say that structuralism is not capable of being just such a caricature), the 'Georges Bataille' we are dealing with *is* such an effect – the controlling device permitting us to surmise the existence of a real Georges Bataille who would be responsible for the texts, the work, the *œuvre*, in front of us. This is why we might wish to refer to a *figure* – it contains the reference both to the person, and to an effect that arises from a text. 'Georges Bataille' is both of these, for us now, and can be regarded as always only having been such a figure.[3] The 'figure' of Georges Bataille contains his 'life and works', but in seeing him as the figure of a real person, we are able to acknowledge the reconstruction, the work, the *œuvre* that is Bataille.

Bataille was born in 1897, in Billom, Puy-de-Dôme, spending much of his childhood in Rheims. His early years were dominated by the descent of his father into the advanced stages of syphilis, and his mother's patience in these years. Bataille makes much of his ... of his father, thinking them to be of crucial signifi-
... *Story of the Eye* ...

progressively more blind, more incontinent, and less capable of associating with the world with anything approaching sanity. Clearly, psychoanalysts would say, here is the root of it all. Bataille himself offers the images of early life in the family as a gesture to psychoanalysis, but how are we to read this self-psychoanalysing? In the context of an appendix to *The Story of the Eye*, might it not be construed as an attack on the discourse of psychoanalysis: if the 'symbols' were always so overt, psychoanalysis would never have 'needed' to exist. Bataille himself did essentially believe that psychoanalysis had something to offer, but his writing continually exceeds the bounds that psychoanalysis hoped to introduce.[4]

Furthermore, given his view that surrealism's project was misplaced if it aimed to bring out and liberate the 'true self' (see, for example, 'The "Old Mole" and the Prefix *Sur* in the Words *Surhomme [Superman]* and *Surrealist*'),[5] could it not be argued that the father evoked is a ready-made myth? The blind, pissing, shitting father undoes psychoanalysis (as nothing is left unconscious, nothing is even mysterious), and the authority it seeks to reinvest in the figure of the father.

The other element of significance in Bataille's early life is his relation to Catholicism, to which he converted in 1914. This phase was marked by a certain asceticism, something he would later (ostensibly) reject. In 1918, from this religious perspective, he wrote 'Notre Dame de Rheims', bemoaning the tragedy of the cathedral having been bombed. Denis Hollier, in *Against Architecture* (3–13, in particular), goes as far as to attribute the rest of Bataille's work to the rejection of this piece, and from this rejection comes the attack on architecture, as a sign (and structure) of organized thought and social systems.[6] Certainly the risibility of the essay would alone account for Bataille's 'forgetting' its existence, but whilst its significance might be largely negative, it does indicate what the 'Catholic Bataille' was thinking. The year 1920 marked the effective end of Bataille's Catholicism (a break which would be definitive by 1923). In the course of attending a seminary on the Isle of Wight, he lost his faith, the void coming to (not) replace the presence of God.

The 1920s were the time of Bataille's encounter with the writings of Nietzsche, and the start of his career as archivist. One of the 'amusing' commonplaces about Bataille is this apparent duality between librarian and writer of pornographic novels (and philosophy that is far stranger than the novels). Even were such a duality representative of Bataille, the ridiculousness of the juxtaposition would not act as a shock to his philosophy, which constantly trades off the profane, mundane world against the moments of the 'other' – of sacrifice, death, transgression and eroticism. According to Surya, in any case, this dualistic image has taken on too great a currency. References to and from Bataille's acquaintances suggest rather that Bataille turned up to work without enthusiasm, and was often absent – because he was 'living his philosophy' of excess most of the time. In a way this is disappointing, as the tension of librarian/would-be transgressor has merely given way to a much more existentialist kind of vision – a vision of someone 'realizing' their philosophy, authentically. Whether Surya is right to move in this direction or not, the question of a certain engagement is at least raised – in terms of the 'putting into practice' of one's thought. Which is as far as this question will be taken, as any belief in any of Bataille's thought renders such questions of authentic behaviour puerile (but puerile is not the same as false or bad . . .).

This period also sees the formation of several important friendships, or relations, at least, with Michel Leiris, André Masson, Boris Souvarine, Raymond Queneau and the surrealists as a group, including a prickly relationship with André Breton. In addition, Bataille was studying under Léon Chestov, who was drawing the links between Nietzsche, Sade and Dostoevsky, as well as with certain elements of Christianity. It is worth noting that for Bataille, this direct community of thought would be something to which he continually philosophically aspired, and which was also ever present, in actuality, throughout his life. Bataille's position as the possible centre of twentieth-century French thought is furthered through these links, whether commentators have chosen to focus on predecessors, peers or descendants. I would argue that some of the links are in practice much more relevant than others, and would

effectively, having taken surrealism too far. Whilst Bataille saw the virtues in aspects of surrealism, he found it useless (a term we will discover to constitute more than a criticism). This is not to say that Bataille cannot be recuperated as part of surrealism (from *The Story of the Eye* to *The Tears of Eros* of 1961, there is a clear valorization of something like surrealism), just that there was no adherence on his part, and no recognition of the *reality* surrealism seemed determined to expose.

The late 1920s are the site of Bataille's first writings, which, from a distance, could be seen as 'surreal'. These are 'Solar Anus' – in which arguably all the 'key ideas' of Bataille are already present; *The Story of the Eye*; and various texts around the idea of 'the pineal eye'.[7] 'Solar Anus' and 'The Pineal Eye' both attempt to introduce ideas of dirt, destruction and eroticism to thought – in a way that ultimately seeks the falling apart of thought. *The Story of the Eye*, written under a pseudonym (Lord Auch), is an amiably narrated tale of the coming together of sensation, death, sex, bodily excretions, blasphemy, the erotic asphyxiation of a priest, and bull's balls.[8] This period also sees Bataille's first involvement in a specifically communal enterprise – the journal *Documents*, which was twisted by Bataille from being a straightforward anthropological-archaeological journal to one that sought to link art and anthropology as ways into a philosophical understanding of the sacred through excessive behaviours and practices. It became something which had an avowed aim in considering certain practices, as opposed to constructing supposedly objective documents.

This involvement with journals (including, in the case of *Documents*, the writing of numerous essays) was to continue in the form of contributions to Boris Souvarine's *La Critique sociale* (a radical left-wing publication) and to *Minotaure* (a surrealist publication). He also founded two groups, in the mid-1930s: the first, Contre-attaque (Counter-attack), was to form a rallying point for dissident communists and leftists (which would resemble Bataille's position, at least at this point). The second was Acéphale (meaning, approximately, the Headless Man. This was the mythical figure that Bataille and Masson came up with to symbolize the ridiculous, unrational, sacrificial man, coming in the wake of the dead god. It can mean headless one, but they do indicate headless *man*). Acéphale was the source of a journal and of a secret society. As a journal, it signalled Bataille's shift to a fully sacrificial, Nietzschean perspective. As a society, little is known of it, except, infamously, that they planned to have a human sacrifice. Apparently there was a willing victim, but no one willing to be the sacrificer.

So, one way of charting Bataille's progress is through these activities. Another consists of seeing the development in terms of intellectual encounters with individuals – and this will bring us round to a further, specific 'joint venture'. The 1930s were marked by meetings with various of the principal actors in French intellectual life at the time (and later). Bataille met, and was close to, the following: Roger Caillois, Simone Weil, Jacques Lacan, Pierre Klossowski and Walter Benjamin. The first focal point was the course given by Alexandre Kojève – who effectively reintroduced Hegel to French thought. By the mid-1930s, it could be said that Bataille's ideas were crystallizing around those of Nietzsche and Mauss, along with Kojève's Hegel, while taking in Marx and Sade. This period saw the appearance of major essays such as 'The Notion of Expenditure', which began to systematize the idea of excess while challenging the idea of system. Although this essay is arguably the base for the 'more developed' elements of Bataille's thought, one of the particularities of his writing is that there are numerous start and end points, as well as many possible central notions. Both at the level of the content of the essays produced and that of the theories within them we can see the irreducibility of the 'system' – it cannot be formed into a genuine system, but everywhere you look there are points of linkage (see Chapter 1

Other essays produced at the time (which could also be seen as equally, paradoxically, formative) include essays on Nietzsche, emphasizing the incompatibility of his thought with Fascism, essays on Fascism in general, on Sade, on access and the status of art (see *Visions of Excess* for a representative sample) . . . or *OC* I and II. . . . . . he wrote *The Blue of Night* (which would appear in

culmination of this period in the shape of the Collège de Sociologie, which brought together many of the names cited above, in a bid to think and create something of the 'sacred community' that was occurring in their texts. The principal actors were Bataille, Leiris and Caillois, but eventually Bataille was left alone, presiding over its ending. Bataille had gone too far theoretically, and not far enough practically, seems to have been the view (of everyone but Bataille). The last lecture of the college (entitled 'The College of Sociology'), however, shows that Bataille had, up to now, been holding back. Here, finally, he sought to combine the erotic, the sacrificial, the idea of community, death and the gift, but without supplying a synthesis or a programme.

Another trajectory through the 1930s remains: the one that features 'Laure', the pseudonym of Colette Peignot. Bataille had been married, to Sylvia (who would later marry Lacan), and had a daughter, Laurence. In 1934 he began an intense affair with Colette Peignot, who shared and inspired many of Bataille's predilections. Her writings, and Bataille's comments on them, show that she was not simply cast as a muse, but that both were actively pursuing loss of identity through the love and death of eroticism and degradation.[9] Peignot, however, was seemingly more affected by these descents than Bataille, and succumbed to illness, dying in 1938 – the very real death at the core of Bataille's wartime writings (and thus another provisional beginning).

The second world war saw no active involvement on Bataille's part. He alternated between illness, quasi-existential philosophical research, and the maintenance of an everyday reality. In many ways, for all of his writing of the great conflagrations of sacrifice and death, it was as if the war were not occurring.[10] In terms of writing, the war is marked by what would become the 'Somma Atheologica', comprising *Inner Experience*, *Guilty* and *On Nietzsche*, among other texts. There are hints of war in *Guilty*, and in the slightly later novel *L'Abbé C*, but principally the texts of this period address the question of the subject – of the loss of the subject in a 'deep subjectivity', which is precisely nothing. Bataille was seeking to confront this emptiness in a way that undid the attempt at mastery that is present in such a confrontation (as in existentialism, which tries to live with it). This period shows Bataille as being as close to the idea of a project (of there being means to attain certain ends, in life, in philosophy) as he ever is – even if to disavow it, even if this project is to be the loss of projectness.

Sartre attacked *Inner Experience*, and echoed Breton's earlier attack, which was to the effect that Bataille 'needed help', as he was fatally obsessed with all that was unpleasant and dangerous, and above (or below) all, he did not supply any hope in the form of a project.[11] Sartre also attacked Bataille's mysticism. By means of reply, Bataille writes in *The Accursed Share*:

> the author of this book on economy is situated (by a part of his work) in the line of mystics of all times (but he is nonetheless far removed from all the presuppositions of the various mysticisms, to which he opposes only the lucidity of *self-consciousness*). (197n.; *OC* VII, 179n.)

This statement is highly important, as it indicates that Bataille regards all thought as mystical – but that which has been seen as mystical is to be regarded as better than philosophy that would be taught as a discipline for reason alone.[12]

The period of the war is also marked by Bataille's heightened friendship with Maurice Blanchot, a friendship that occurred through work on similar projects and by their establishing a system of mutual commentary, as well as at the more personal level. Both writers, strange though it may at first seem (for writers who seemingly valorize the negative), come to value the sense of community that emerges from shared intellectual projects, and the role such a community plays in exceeding the necessarily restricted nature of the individual subject, taken alone.[13]

key to all his ideas (it being the elucidation of the notion of general economy). Along with two further volumes, which were unpublished in his lifetime, this work brings together the concerns about the nothingness that informs subjectivity, about sacrifice and expenditure as the principle behind life and society, and about how such concerns can be thought through a double context of philosophy and political realities.[14] The linchpin in all of this was Mauss's theory of the gift – in Bataille's hands now something violent and sacrificial. At the same time, Bataille was working on the *Theory of Religion*, which came out posthumously. In this text Bataille addresses the transfer of the sacred into a realm managed by religion – such that religion can come to be seen as being effectively part of the profane world, ejecting what it fears.

Through the 1950s, in the published works, at least, art is granted more of a central place than before, even if not a consistent one. Whilst Bataille had been continually interested in, and had written on, art, it was only now that it became a clear part of the heterogeneous system that was building up (although not building into anything). The principal works of this time are on the cave paintings at Lascaux, and on Manet. Other major texts were being written at this time: as well as the continually reworked volumes of *The Accursed Share*, Bataille wrote *Literature and Evil* and *Eroticism*, both of which came out in 1957. The first of these is probably the most straightforward of Bataille's book-length works (although to be more precise, it is a collection of thematically linked essays that first appeared in *Critique*). It is a particular sort of literary criticism, selecting various writers (from Brontë to Sade) and identifying how the forbidden, the dangerous, or 'the other' emerges in their writing. The longest essay, on Genet, is largely an attack on Sartre's belief in living life as a project, as presented in *Saint Genet*. For Bataille, what is interesting in Genet is precisely not that – he regards Genet's life and works as a specific attack on all ideas of coherent end-oriented living (which makes everything else into merely means) itself. *Eroticism* is no more or less about eroticism than any of his other texts – which have been combining eroticism, death, social analysis, science, pseudo-science, myth and politics into a totality that disperses itself. *Eroticism* is very much within Bataille's notion of the general economy – where expenditure and waste combine with, and in, death and the erotic. In a way that is 'reminiscent' of Foucault in his *History of Sexuality*, sex is not 'the erotic', but the policed form of eroticism. Like Foucault, Bataille does not advocate 'sexual liberation' – the erotic is what would alternately seep into and explode through the taboos, *not* what would abolish them.[15]

The remaining years are ones of extreme illness (respiratory and rheumatic), and a gradual loss of contact with the world. The periods of illness were intermittent, and according to Surya, this alternation between absence, pain and lucid awareness only served to reinforce Bataille's philosophy (*La Mort à l'œuvre*, 577). Whatever the value of such an observation, we can see the textual evidence in *The Tears of Eros*, which was painfully compiled over three years, and came out in 1961.[16] This work is a history of art that, in Bataille's view, approaches the sacred, as it exceeds mere depiction, stimulating reactions that go beyond reason (as with pornography, or horror films). It includes, amongst others, cave paintings, mannerism, surrealism, and pictures of a Chinese man being dismembered. In this book, we can see the aspiration of a limited form (for art, read also the subject individual) to leave itself behind, through the invocation of horror. Bataille's *Tears of Eros* is a rewriting of his postwar theorizations, and seems to be an attempt to bring everything together once more, this time via art. The attempt is less than successful – he seems to be leaving words behind, leaving them to their failure.

The pictures of the Chinese man had a long history for Bataille,

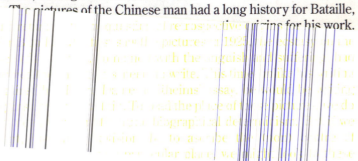

Alternatively, we might keep in mind a combination of his erotic interests, Hegel, Nietzsche, Mauss, Sade, surrealism and 'transgressive' art, as being the principal elements 'behind' the *œuvre*. For we who come now, Bataille's positioning as 'pre-poststructuralist' must be included, and the text we come to has come through Derrida, Foucault, Kristeva and Baudrillard at least as much as 'from' its precursors. Acknowledging our lateness in the reading of what leads to Bataille, we nonetheless need to approach the textual origins – i.e. those writers who appear within Bataille's texts as their progenitors.

The first chapter of this book brings three of these points of influence together. In asking the question, 'Does Bataille have a system?' we have to consider the various systems that emerge in Hegel, Sade and Durkheim. Bataille does have something like a system, but if it is one, it also includes the attempt to get away from systematic philosophy. The name that this 'non-system' might have is the 'general economy', an idea that underpins the three volumes of *The Accursed Share*. Chapter 2 works through the first volume of this series to examine and account for the workings of Bataillean notions of waste, excess, squander, expenditure.

Chapter 3 looks at the place of death in the general economy, and focuses on the second volume of *The Accursed Share*, introducing his conception of abjection, and how this, in combination with his particular take on death, requires us to think about his view of women's position. Chapter 4 centres on the final volume of *The Accursed Share*, and deals with sovereignty: how the general economy works in and through the individual. The links between sovereignty and 'inner experience' are also pursued, as is the relationship between sovereignty and writing.

Chapter 5 explores Bataille's thought of community, which revolves around sacrifice, possibly in the form of human sacrifice, but can also entail loss of the self in the festival, or in eroticism. In *Eroticism* Bataille uses the term 'continuity' to designate this 'community' with the other, and the link into eroticism leads us to the next chapter, which looks at eroticism in terms of transgression. The notion of abjection is re-examined, as is the possibility of a more generalized view of transgression. Both Chapters 5 and 6, and particularly the latter, address Bataille's fictional texts. Chapter

7 investigates Bataille's views on art and aesthetics, and how these fit in with his other theoretical predilections. Art becomes increasingly significant in his writings of the 1950s, which are a more cohesive version of his early writings on art (although Bataille is not always keen to have achieved such a thing). Chapter 8 deals with Bataille's political, ultra-leftist views from before the war, and his views on political action before and after the war, including his disgust at the heroic commitment (*engagement*) of French intellectuals, particularly Sartre. In the closing few pages, I end with Bataille's desire for silence, his incessant writing always in the knowledge that silence was impossible, is the impossible.

Notes

1. Habermas, even if critical of both Bataille and much contemporary French thought, is one of the first to signal the pervasive importance of Bataille in the latter. See 'The French Path to Postmodernity', which first appears in *New German Critique*, 33 (Fall, 1984): 79–102.

2. Surya starts from a presumption that Bataille's writing is heavily autobiographical, and can essentially be relied upon to be accurate in this. At two points he hesitates (La Mort à l'œuvre, 22, 64), but the rest of Bataille's life seems to come from *OC* I, III, V and VI. The wartime period in particular is culled from *OC* V and VI (*La Mort à l'œuvre*, 331–434). Clearly, as an intellectual biography, much is going to emerge from a consideration of the writings, but Surya's text wishes to be seen as representing facts about Bataille's life, and only a closer inspection reveals that much is taken straight from the fictional or semi-fictional texts. Such *textual* construction makes Surya a post- structuralist biographer, despite himself.

claim that some 'primitive' societies even have their unconscious where it can be seen (and hence used for 'our' myth-making).

6. Hollier's text is a sustained reading of Bataille from this perspective of the attack on building, constructing, conserving. Bataille's 'Notre Dame de Rheims' is included in this volume (15–19) (*OC* I, 611–16).

7. See 'The Jésuve', and 'The Pineal Eye'. These are part of the 'Dossier de l'œil pinéal' (*OC* II, 13–47). For a range of Bataille's writings on surrealism, art and intellectual movements, see *The Absence of Myth: Writings on Surrealism*, and *OC* II, XI and XII.

8. The English edition comes safely packaged with Sontag's essay on the differences between the erotic and the pornographic ('The Pornographic Imagination', 83–118), and Barthes's attempt to limit the story to being a chain of metaphor ('The Metaphor of the Eye', 119–27). Both are satisfactory readings, but here perform the role of validation rather than that of actually supplementing Bataille's 'story'.

9. See *Laure: The Collected Writings*. See also Bataille, *Guilty*. The other relationship to be noted is the one with Diane Koutchoubey, which started in 1943, and lasted until Bataille's death (they were married in 1951). It should not be surmised from this short listing that Bataille was either monogamous or a partisan of marriage or of lasting relationships as such.

10. Bataille's position on war would seem ambivalent, although it will become clear in later works that war is the rendering useful of the sacred realm of death and sacrifice. Before the war, he could range from his warnings about Fascism and war, and the need for some form of revolution (if not 'the' revolution) in 'Contre-attaque' ('Dossier de contre-attaque'; for all his contributions to this grouping, see *OC* I, 379–432) to the following: 'I MYSELF AM WAR. I imagine human movement and excitation, whose possibilities are limitless: this movement and excitation can only be appeased by war. I imagine the gift of infinite suffering.' ('The Practice of Joy before Death', 239). This latter text dates from the 'Acéphale' period, and could be construed as a shift – but the case could be made that Bataille is talking about two different types of war: one in the real world, another 'symbolic'. Bataille does gesture towards a reconciliation of these 'two types of war', in *Guilty* (51–8) (*OC* V, 289–97), through a consideration of how he is living the war, and how non-involvement is both better than fighting, and more base (hence the guilt).

11. Sartre, 'Un Nouveau mystique' ('A New Mystic') in *Situations I*, 143–88. As for Breton before him, it is clear that, for Sartre, Bataille was enough of a threat to receive substantial criticism. In fact, much of what Sartre says is apt, but this does not stop him missing the essential point that all the things he identifies are the point of the book, not symptoms of some other cause.

12. See also 'Méthode de méditation'(*OC* V, 191–228), where he distinguishes himself from Heidegger in the following terms: 'I am not a philosopher, but a saint, maybe a madman' (217n.).

13. See Bataille, *Inner Experience*, 7 (*OC* V, 19) and Blanchot's later work (such as *The Infinite Conversation*, and *The Unavowable Community*, much of which is written as active retrospection on the multiple layers of (impossible) community. See also Jean-Luc Nancy, *The Inoperative Community*.

14. The later volumes appear in one book as *The Accursed Share*, vols II and III. The individual titles are *The History of Eroticism* (*OC* VIII, 7–165), and *Sovereignty* (*OC* VIII, 243–456).

15. On the specific question of taboo and transgression in Bataille, see also Foucault, 'Preface to Transgression', in *Language, Counter-Memory and Practice*, 29–52.

16. Bataille also produced in *The Trial of Gilles de Rais* (the trial itself being translated by Pierre Klossowski) an edition of the trial of Gilles de Rais, including an accompanying essay. How we see Gilles de Rais is in some ways the embodiment of Bataille's philosophy: a monster but sacred.

1

System

All of Bataille's book-length works announce themselves through the statement of what, for Bataille, is a necessary paradox: how can a text claim to be against the accumulation of knowledge, the furthering of a project and so on, when its mere existence suggests the opposite? In other words, Bataille is constantly faced with the question of how he can write what he wants to write, when this seeks to be an anti-writing. Bataille finds himself in a position familiar to Beckett – the impossibility of words combined with the impossibility of silence. *The Accursed Share*, *Eroticism*, *Inner Experience* and *Theory of Religion* all start from this position – a position which serves as an undermining of his own project at the same time as it serves as a statement of intent. In *The Accursed Share*, he writes:

> writing this book in which I was saying that energy finally can only be wasted, I myself was using my energy, my time, working; my research answered in a fundamental way the desire to add to the amount of wealth acquired for mankind. Should I say that under these conditions I sometimes could only respond to the truth of my book and not go on writing it? (11; *OC* VII, 20–1)

Is there a way of incorporating this problem into a consideration of the theory itself? In writing on, Bataille offers the strange possibility that not only is there a paradox, but this paradox is in some way the *proof*, the verification of the perversity of the universe Bataille identifies. He also installs something like a system. Though he writes in a way that is anti-systemic and anti-systematic, the notion of system *is* what links the highly diverse influences Bataille claims for himself.

In *Theory of Religion*, we see the concern with the impossibility of writing (on certain subjects), the concern not to be engaged in the pursuit of a fixed project, and we also see an explicit list of writers Bataille cites as the sources of this (and other) works. These sections frame the text proper, and will also serve as the frame here. The selection of the late text *Theory of Religion* is not an arbitrary one, but a recognition that by the stage of its writing, Bataille has the concern about writing a coherent and *useful* theory well honed, and also, more crucially for us here, he actually cites his 'predecessors'.[1] The presence of Hegel, Nietzsche and Mauss is all-pervasive in Bataille's *œuvre*, but is not always made explicit. Here it is almost too overt for readers and writers schooled against the 'intentionist fallacy' (although Nietzsche is not referred to).[2] After an analysis of the frame of *Theory of Religion* comes a consideration of the specific relevance of Hegel, Sade, Durkheim and Mauss, in terms of their *systems*, in order to see what kind of a system – if any – emerges in Bataille. His term 'heterology', ostensibly derived in order to describe Sade's work, and representing all that cannot fit into a system, is effectively a statement of his own theoretical intent, and serves here as a point of reference to define the contours of Bataille's theories.

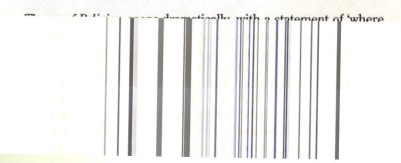

separate, writing being about separation. Grandiose statements, such as that cited above, are as common in Bataille as they are in Nietzsche, and as with the latter, they are to be undermined and prevented from being *realizable* truths (or presentation of same), as 'in a sense the unlimited assemblage is the impossible' (*Theory of Religion*, 9; *OC* VII, 285).[3] The text itself, though, is not to address the impossible directly (even if it constitutes its content and form) – but is to end up there. In this way, the text functions against itself, destroying its claims, such that 'in this gathering place, where violence is rife, at the boundary of that which escapes cohesion, he who reflects within cohesion realizes that there is no longer any room for him' (10; 285).[4] Destruction has to be brought into an edifice – and, as we shall see, this is why Bataille persists with Hegel, whose writing is taken as a summit from which to fall, a summit that also collapses as this fall occurs (see Hollier, *Against Architecture*, 3–13 and *passim*).

What also unites Bataille and Hegel is the insistence on a 'mobile thought' (11; 287), but, unlike Hegel, who has Spirit realizing itself at (or as) the end of time, for Bataille, 'every point, at each point, there is the impossibility of the final state' (11; 287). In other words, Bataille writes *as if* building towards an end, all the time conscious that this end is to undo itself. Bataille hesitates to call himself a philosopher, and in *Theory of Religion* he writes that philosophy as a discipline is fundamentally limited if it thinks it will get answers in remaining a discipline. Instead, philosophy is to be an adjunct to the 'irresolvable exigency' to be (12; 287). A further theme emerges from this, as this exigency is without limits – so the thought of Being must also know no limits, demand no answer (at least not in the expectation of its arrival): 'so it is an act of consciousness, while carrying one's elucidation to the limit of immediate possibilities, not to seek a definitive state that will never be granted' (12; 288).

This combination of thought as will, and as part of consciousness that evolves, is already to be found in Hegel. Where Bataille differs from Hegel is that the whole structure of this evolving consciousness is meaningless at its end – and this end, like Hegel's, permeates the whole. The complicity of the writer in (or with) writing as process also moves Bataille beyond Hegel, or for example,

Heidegger – beyond professional philosophers who manage to keep thought/writing as a controllable object, perhaps despite their own theories.[5]

Another similarity to Hegel is in the consideration Bataille gives to the individual as being caught within community. There are differences that go beyond simple nuancing, but in Bataille's statement that 'there cannot be any philosophy of the individual and the exercise of thought cannot have any other outcome than the negation of individual perspectives' (13; 288) we see the more active, even nihilistic sense in which Bataille says 'the same' as Hegel. Bataille rejects existentialism's voluntaristic take on phenomenology and reiterates the community of existence as both realization and annulling of the individual.

As we will see in his 'general economy', Bataille regards any valorization of the individual as a reduction of humans to things. This 'thingness' of the individual is a recurrent idea in Bataille, and is more than the individual's alienation from their 'true self' – rather, it is the alienation that constitutes the individual: the individual *is* alienation, negation and death. Religion also reduces humans to things, as we come to serve ends beyond ourselves. Religion, then, which ostensibly seeks to rescue us, is not to be seen as the way of uniting 'Man' with what is beyond, but as the desperate, mortal attempt to control and dispose of this beyond which Bataille will label the sacred – *in opposition* to religion.[6]

The individual writer is not exempt from this communal existence that constitutes his or her belief in their individuality ('the foundation of one's thought is the thought of another' [9; 285]). In

In the first place, the work is to be seen as a product of prior texts, and most interestingly, this is to be done 'after the event'. With the first element, we have a form of what is now habitually called intertextuality, and with the second, one of the many pre-emptings Bataille makes of Derrida's theories: that of the retrospective attribution of origins, such that they were 'always already' there.

At a more direct level, Bataille cites the importance of various sociological and anthropological writers – such as Georges Dumézil, Max Weber, R. H. Tawney, Durkheim, Mauss and Kojève (122–7; 358–61). I would draw particular attention to the last three of these, and for the moment, concentrate on Kojève, who is known principally for his *Introduction to the Reading of Hegel*.[7] Bataille stresses the importance of Kojève's work for his own, in terms of how the latter has managed to bring out and expand on Hegel's *Phenomenology of Spirit* (*Theory of Religion*, 124; *OC* VII, 359). The main points raised by Kojève are the following: firstly, he alters (or perhaps clarifies) the emphasis, making death the centre of Hegel's system. Secondly, he manages to account for the system that occurs within *Phenomenology of Spirit*. Thirdly, and crucially for Bataille, 'Kojéve's interpretation does not deviate in any way from Marxism' (124; 359). This observation is important because it moves us from the supposed idealism of Hegel. Furthermore, it illustrates to us the importance Bataille attributed to bringing together thoughts of the everyday economy-based world and what lies, or is seen to lie, beyond.[8]

With death now repositioned, or perhaps occupying the position it always (already) occupied, we need to look at Kojève's account of Hegel's system. It is often presumed that a system is something external to its elements, insofar, at least, as it organizes them. Hegel's systematic approach would then simply consist of the fact that he tried to create a system wherein all could be accounted for – hence works on aesthetics, science, religion, philosophy, history, politics – everything. According to Kojève, Hegel's notion of system is much more than this.[9] The system consists of the importance of death, which structures everything else, but (the) system is also to be seen as the means of truth (see *Introduction*, 532–3).

Hegel writes 'that the True is actual only as system, or that Substance is essentially Subject, is expressed in the representation of the Absolute as *Spirit* – the most sublime Notion and the one which belongs to the modern age and its religion' (*Phenomenology of Spirit*, 14). Now, Hegel is at least partly referring to himself, as he takes his writing to necessarily occupy a historical point along a path of progress in thought and Being (these two adding, approximately, to Spirit), but as well as this, truth can only come about as part of a dynamic – so the system is not static, but is systematic movement – something we will see in Bataille's conceptualizations, particularly that of the general economy.

At this point we need to look more directly at Hegel. Firstly, the term 'Notion' – this is something that is thought 'in Spirit' (i.e. something that features in the progress toward ultimate understanding through self-consciousness) and is necessarily dynamic, a process of becoming (see *Phenomenology of Spirit*, 7, 20). Bataille uses the term 'notion' in preference to the more static term of concept (a procedure also followed by Derrida). The term 'Spirit' is more or less equivalent to self-consciousness, and the term 'Substance' to that which is not self-consciousness. However, the specific advance Hegel makes is that these seemingly opposed ideas become interdependent, with one adding meaning to the other, through a process of 'negativity'. In order to understand the processes of Bataille's theories, this idea of negativity in *its creation of a system*, has to be addressed.

Kojève points to the centrality of death in Hegel's thought, particularly in *Phenomenology of Spirit*. Death is the negativity *par excellence*, but due to the importance of process, and the interaction of seemingly opposed elements, it is not as simple as that

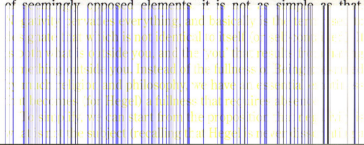

world (*Phenomenology of Spirit*, 21), Substance (33), language (66), Nature (177–8), in the master/slave relation (111–18), in law and community (225), work (242–6), Absolute Being (323), reason (344), morality (368) and in death in the form of the sacrificed Son of God (470–1). Spirit is a result of negativity (485), and the Self, in the end, is a relation only of difference, of 'absolute negativity' (489). It is to be remembered that whilst initially language, community, objects and so on are in opposition to the individual, this opposition is overcome, so that awareness of negativity constitutes the subject, and only such coming to awareness (of the dynamic and negative character of Being) is true.

The principal negativity remains death, however. This might seem obvious, but what is notable is the constructive role death plays in creating the possibility of self-aware individuals and humanity. For Hegel, to be human is to be aware of death – and this is precisely why Spirit must overcome – i.e. annul but maintain – the power of death (19). The individual ejects death, making it external – thus creating the very movement that will make the individual into a subject. Death is separated in order to bring it back in domesticated fashion, now part of the known world (see Kojève, *Introduction*, 546). In a slightly less abstract way, Hegel refers to the master/slave relation (*Phenomenology of Spirit*, 111–18), which is for many (notably Marx) the introduction of a recognizable historical dimension. History is seen, in this light, as the struggle for recognition that 'I' am a subject. This entails either the death of the other, or the other's metaphorical death and enslavement. This battle requires risking death, for you might end up the loser. Whatever the outcome, death is banished to the profit of life based on recognition (114).[10] Death is also overcome in the development of work – as the conscious encounter with the other (242–6). Finally, the death of the 'Son of God' rescues not only humans, but also God, from death (471, 475).

What is essential is that death is overcome, thus placing it retrospectively as the driving force of Being. This is what allows Kojève to claim that, for Hegel, man is 'death incarnate' (*Introduction*, 567). This conception, in itself, and as structuring notion, is vital to Bataille's thought. Where Bataille will principally diverge from Hegel is that he does not accept that overcoming death and negativity is the final aim – especially if this is to occur through work and utility (Hegel's preferred solution at the historical stage he writes in), even if he does accept that this is, in practice, what we do.

Sade does not feature in the list of 'influences' in *Theory of Religion*, but makes frequent appearances in Bataille's texts, from early articles bemoaning surrealism's simplistic reading of him – limiting Sade to the status of literary exponent of sexual freedom ('The Use Value of D.A.F. de Sade'), through *The Accursed Share*, vols II and III, to *Eroticism* and *Literature and Evil*. Following on from the negativity offered by Hegel, it might almost seem obvious to mention Sade, who is renowned for accounts of the infliction of pain and death. Bataille, however, is one of the first to emphasize Sade's *utter* philosophical aspect. For Bataille, philosophy must go to its limit, and in this light Sade attains a limit *systematically*, in the same way as Hegel seeks to attain a conceptualization of final, perfected Being in self-consciousness. Bataille picks up not only on the extreme nature of Sade's writing, but on how this fits with a rigorous, tortuous system.

Everyone 'knows' about Sade's works, and that they consist of catalogues of brutality – leading to the contemporary use of the word 'sadism'. At another level, he is taken to be an advocate of (sexual) liberation, and will help free us from our neuroses. Still another reading seeks to investigate Sade as philosopher. Bataille starts from this last perspective, but not to the detriment of the reiterations of violent sexuality essential to Sade's system completion, as it is always *against* (18–19), and therefore does not establish what used to be wrong or criminal as a new law. Sade shares with Hegel the notion of overcoming, although in the former's case it is a pure overcoming of even the self. Whilst we might wish to style Sade's view as 'negative dialectics', perhaps he is in fact following exactly the same model as Hegel, but for Sade there is to be no positive outcome from negativity. At another level, Sade gives us another dialectic, which moves from Man against God, through Man against Nature, to Man against his own self. It is a dialectical process as each element contains part of its opposite – if Man is free or evil, then this is due either to God or to God's absence, and/or if Man is cruel, acting against Nature, this is because nature has made him so (*Sade My Neighbour*, 99–102), and eventually, the only place left after this is the destruction of self in apathy. So at every stage, the acting against is part of acting positively – as in the creation of God, Nature, humanity.

Klossowski's powerful reading of Sade is a more overt version of Bataille's use of Sade (Bataille refers extensively to Klossowski in *Literature and Evil*), but seems to miss a final dimension, one that will be seen to tie in with Bataille's notion of the general economy. Klossowski almost entirely neglects accumulation as a process (even though 'quantity' is the way to apathy: *Sade My Neighbour*, 34), in favour of a more profound dialectic. The accumulation and dialectic can perhaps better be seen as also acting in a dialectical relationship: i.e. Sade's system itself is also double.

This double system can be seen at work in *The 120 Days of Sodom*. The 120 days in question are to be strictly regulated: the four 'libertines' are to hear 600 stories in total (150 simple passions, 150 complex passions, 150 criminal passions, 150 murderous passions), with the four only allowed to engage in particular acts after they have been the subject of a story (this enactment generally providing the moral of the story . . .). The stories start as very uncomplicated accounts, and move through an array of 'variations', with each story to get more extreme as they go on, thus fuelling the desire of the libertines, while annulling it; this annulling is continually demonstrated, as after a while only the most recent, most extreme acts will do.

Various other rules pertain, replacing divine or State law. These rules apply, for example, to which group of people is to be used for which tasks, services or acts, and when. Certain acts are to be committed out of view. Sade also lists the participants, how they were selected, and what their role will be (the list is given twice, once in a form designed for the reader's 'easy reference'). At the end, a balance sheet is given, detailing the numbers killed, those who survived and so on. There is an increased vehemence to the acts, following the pattern of the stories, combined with much in the way of moral comment – as to the virtues of 'vice' for example; but eventually, as the days wear on, the acts themselves are praised simply as autonomous acts (it is perhaps significant that three of the four sections are little more than lists).

This all sits well with Klossowski's definition of Sade as a dialectical moralist of sorts, but the sheer accumulation should also be seen as *just* that (paradoxical though such a statement is). The volume of attacks that eventually exceed pleasures that are sexually (end-)oriented is significant as a brute fact, because this is precisely the apathy Klossowski is writing about, wherein the moral question is lost, and all we have is a list, an enumeration of acts. This other facet of Sade's system provides a model which is one of increase, of addition but not of qualitative change. This dual system (dialectic/accumulation) annuls the dialectic altogether, and instead we might call the model one of excess and accumulation. This then serves as one possible derivation of Bataille's notion of general economy.

A further contribution to the bases of Bataille's writing comes from

composite picture at any given point. Essential to any such idea is that nothing is outside of society (or analysis) – that everything to do with humans emerges from society. Whilst things such as nature, God, the soul, etc. might exist, they have no human meaning until socially mediated (if not created): 'from the fact that the ideas of time, space, class, cause or personality are constructed out of social elements, it is not necessary to conclude that they are devoid of all objective value' (*Elementary Forms*, 19).

Society creates social facts, and 'what constitutes social facts are the beliefs, tendencies and practices of the group taken collectively' (*The Rules of Sociological Method*, 54). Social facts, then, are not any old facts, but the mediating devices of 'brute facts' that (a) society evolves, *as seen* by the sociologist ('*taken* collectively'). The observer is necessary, to see society in this form. Even with regular admissions of this 'need to be observed', Durkheim does believe that his objectivity is not as socially constructed as that of 'primitive peoples' (a term he uses very carefully, if still in a way we might distrust today [see *Elementary Forms*, 1–8]), and that they too are engaged in their own processes of classification, 'and if the totality of things is conceived as a single system, this is because society itself is seen in the same way. It is a whole, or rather it is *the* unique whole to which everything is related' (Durkheim and Mauss, *Primitive Classification*, 83). Durkheim's point is ostensibly that primitive societies themselves see things in this way, which could be construed as problematic, as it attributes his own society's structure of thinking to another. It is certainly presumptuous, and, in any case, what remains is still the necessity for someone to be able to see the whole, and therefore be outside.

In *Primitive Classification*, Durkheim and Mauss are concerned with the totality of specific societies. Elsewhere, Durkheim addresses a particular phenomenon (labour, suicide, religion), as does Mauss (magic, sacrifice, the gift) as a totality – the data from 'primitive societies' are seen as capable of providing generalizable answers. This is certainly an attitude held by Bataille, although, interestingly, his more cavalier approach to objectivity and facts makes him less ideologically limited to his immediate historical context than Durkheim.[11]

These two approaches, which serve to create complete systems, combine in a further definition given by Durkheim of the social fact. He reiterates the element of constraint (i.e. the construction of obligation or prohibition), and then goes on to unite the systems of a particular social system with that of a particular social phenomenon (which up until now has itself been seen as a combination of such phenomena), in the following formulation: '[a social fact is a fact] which is general over the whole of a given society whilst having an existence of its own, independent of its individual manifestations' (*The Rules of Sociological Method*, 59). This idea is further developed by Mauss, becoming the 'total social fact'.

The 'total social fact' that emerges in Mauss, from Durkheim, is the manifestation of the 'horizontal system' in Bataille. In his work, this combines with the systems we see at work in Hegel and Sade, providing the link to social phenomena that the other two do not realize as a link, even if such phenomena are present within the individual systems. These developments are what lie between Durkheim's *Elementary Forms* and Bataille's *Theory of Religion*.[12]

How then do these varied inputs come together, and how far can we talk about Bataille's 'system'? Whilst Bataille is as critical of systems as he is of the practice of academic philosophy, this becomes clear only through his elaboration of a systemic logic. Such a systemic logic emerges in his early articles, and bears the name of heterology. Although the term falls out of use in his later texts, its *logic* persists. 'Heterology' coined by Bataille, is 'the science of what is completely other' ('The Use Value of D.A.F. de Sade', 102n.; *OC* II, 61n.).

Heterology, then, stands for the way of looking at what i

which by definition is applicable to homogeneous elements. Above all, heterology is opposed to any homogeneous representation of the world, in other words, to any philosophical system. [. . .] [Heterology] leads to the complete reversal of the philosophical process, which ceases to be an instrument of appropriation, and now serves excretion; it introduces the demand for the violent gratifications implied by social life. ('The Use Value of D.A.F. de Sade', 97; *OC* II, 62–3)

Bataille is caught in the trap of having to describe systematically how he is going to write against systems – and as we have seen, his introductions show us that he is aware of this. This awareness is what underlies Bataille's maintenance of Hegel as his 'other': like Sade, Bataille cannot simply write or act 'positively', autonomously – as this would imply the possibility of being a self-aware, untroubled individual Subject – but myths of organization (truth, the Subject, the system) are to persist as 'true' in order that the *other* myths of excess, of destruction, violence and abjection can be brought into the light, as other (unlike the surrealists, who seek to bring into the light in order to cure us of society's ills).

For Bataille, other, 'primitive' societies provide the key, as many of them managed an existence which allowed for regular interruption, irruption and eruption of the sacred as violence (see particularly *The Accursed Share*). Durkheim too had looked to 'primitive societies' to find the key to religious practices as systemic social phenomena, but Bataille seeks to analyse these phenomena at a level untouched by Durkheim, insofar as the latter is content to observe and explain, rather than overtly construct arguments based on his 'findings'. It is from Durkheim (and later, Caillois) that Bataille develops his use of the word sacred, and of the term heterology (coming from Durkheim's use of heterogeneity). Durkheim sees a profound difference between the sacred and the profane, whilst Bataille sees the process of rendering them as different as the element of heterogeneity. Compare Bataille's rendering of 'heterogeneous' with Durkheim:

But if a purely hierarchical distinction is a criterium [sic] at once too general and too imprecise, there is nothing left with which to characterize the sacred in its relation to the profane except their heterogeneity. However, this heterogeneity is sufficient to characterize this classification of things and to distinguish it from all others, because it is very particular: *it is absolute*. (Durkheim, *Elementary Forms*, 38)

For Bataille, the split is indeed absolute, but the idea of absoluteness is one firmly within homogeneity; heterogeneity is what breaks what is held to be absolute – it is that which transgresses. A similar divide exists in the division of the sacred world into pure (what is holy) and impure (what is damned or evil). Durkheim fits these categories into a hierarchy of sacredness (*Elementary Forms*, 301–2), whilst Bataille ranges them together in their capacity to threaten the profane world (which exists as a product of the expulsion of the sacred, whether pure or impure), and argues that Sade provides us with the means to see this relation. Bataille rewrites the relation of sacred/profane as '*heterogeneous* (strongly polarized) and *homogeneous* (weakly polarized)' to emphasize that what threatens is anything that is other, and uncategorizable in normal ways (*OC* II, 167).[13] For Durkheim, the heterogeneity is stasis and separation, for Bataille it is that which is outside, but also the process by which it came to be outside, and by which it can come back in again (in sacrifice, for example, or the festival).

So Bataille provides an *abnormal* system for thinking what is outside of the norms, outside of the profane world of work. This '"abnormal" system' could be that of Sade, and also the undoing Bataille adds to Sade. Bataille uses heterology and heterogeneity to provide an unstable systemic logic, which brings together, without homogenizing, the multiple sources in his theory. It is not enough to state that Bataille is against systems – he is against them in a way that undoes, rather than ignores, the logic of systems.

impossible' is more than a statement of the impossibility of completion; it is also a statement that what lies at the end (which is unattainable) is that which is beyond thought, or beyond rational thought at least.

4. Note also that this combination of 'the impossible' *as* impossible specifically takes place *outside* the text, in a (re)playing of the impossibility of the statement of the impossible within the text. This positioning 'recalls' the work of Derrida, in particular 'Parergon' (*The Truth in Painting*, 15–147), which deals with the structure of frames and framing, such that what frames is an integral part of what it is supposedly external to.

5. Adorno would dispute this characterization of Hegel. In *Hegel: Three Studies*, he argues that despite presumptions about his 'bourgeois Idealism', Hegel was living his philosophy (48–51, 120–2). An essential difference remains, as Hegel thereby becomes a proto-existentialist, and the philosopher even more conscious of what he is doing, whereas Bataille's idea is to leave precisely this state of reflection and control of self behind. Loss of the subject in writing is part of this.

6. See *Theory of Religion*, 109–10; *OC* VII, 349, and also 'The Use Value of D.A.F. de Sade', 97; *OC* II, 61), where he writes that '[religion] betrays the needs that it was not only supposed to regulate, but satisfy'.

7. Although this book exists in English, it has been heavily edited, and is missing most of the points to which I refer to here. The page numbers refer to the French text *Introduction à la lecture de Hegel*.

8. Kojève comments on how he sees his reading as something that corrects Heidegger for his lack of historical awareness, and Marx for his lack of a consideration of death (573n.).

9. Adorno is one writer, who whilst recovering Hegel from under the mound of Marxist faint praise, still adheres to this concept that Hegel's system is one because he is systematic (see *Hegel: Three Studies*, 27–40, 146–7).

10. The various paradoxes surrounding this relationship re-emerge in Bataille's notion of sovereignty. See also Kojève, *Introduction*, 14–16, 19–21, on the paradox that it is the slave who, in the long run, attains selfhood, and not the master.

11. See James Clifford, *The Predicament of Culture*, which argues that Bataille (and, to a lesser extent, the surrealists) was engaged in way of thinking that looked to the other *as other* rather than trying to assimilate the other. The problem remains, however, that Bataille uses 'other' cultures as material for generalizable points, and rarely questions his sources.

12. On the contribution of Mauss in this regard, Bataille has this to say:

> Negativity is not 'recognized as such', at the point at which it comes into the game of existence as a stimulus for the major vital responses. Quite the opposite: it is brought into a process of annulment (and here the interpretation of the facts by a sociologist such as Mauss is, for me, of great importance). (*OC* V, 562–3n.)

In other words, Hegel does not investigate the actual processes that structure negativity, but Mauss does. Hegel also neglected the possibility of encountering the sacred in acts of excess, as he sought to live 'reasonably' (*OC* V, 522n.).

13. 'La polarité humaine . . .' ('Human Polarity . . .') (*OC* II, 167). This text is a fragment that features in the 'Dossier "hétérologie"', *OC* II, 165–202. This dossier also includes diagrams of how the heterogeneous acts within and against certain spheres in society, as a transformative, but transient occurrence.

2

General Economy

Heterology persists in Bataille's *œuvre*, but takes the guise of the general economy – a system which seeks to account for what is other (heterogeneous) and to 'be other' in the way it is written (compared to social 'science'). The 'notion of the general economy' emerges in its own right in the essay 'The Notion of Expenditure', which draws together the various strands already at work in Bataille's writing – Hegel, Nietzsche, Sade, anthropology. The ideas announced in this essay are more fully developed throughout the three volumes of *The Accursed Share*, and persist, in a slightly different formulation, in the late texts, such as *Eroticism*. Whilst Bataille's *œuvre* could be categorized as consisting of an array of more or less interchangeable, subtly different terms and notions, this array can be categorized *through* the notion of general economy, which thus comes to serve as the organizing notion of Bataille's work (this organization could be visualized as a set of clusters, or as the contingent constellations of the 'strange attractors' of chaos theory, rather than the linear structures of genuinely systematic philosophies).

The very formulation of something called a 'general economy' suggests an attempt to account for some sort of whole, and also suggests the insufficiency of economics as a free-standing term. In this way, Bataille (from a quasi-Marxist position) challenges the belief held by both capitalism and communism in the primacy of 'the economic', where the economic is the sphere of production, as well as currently being the realm of commodity fetishism. Bataille wishes to criticize a conception of society based on its economics because this categorization is what has led to society being dominated by the economic *sphere*: in other words, the observation that the economic is the most important is not innocent – it has contributed to the problem it 'describes', as it comes from the same set of presumptions.

Bataille argues, via Mauss, that the notion of there being an economic realm that is autonomous is limited to modern, Western, societies, and those brought under their influence,[1] and that to a large extent the economic has no such existence in most societies. Bataille is also echoing Weber, in that he sees capitalism as having removed all vestiges of genuine community and the unifying beliefs of the past (Bataille differs in that, for him, this loss dates from a much earlier period – the start of humanity), as accumulation, and secondarily, profit, have taken over (*The Accursed Share*, 136; *OC* VII, 130). As a result of this privileging of the economic, all value is processed in the same way. In fact, even the idea of value is complicit in this. The result is that what is valued is all that fosters accumulation and preservation, or comes from them. Bataille's general economy seeks to get beyond this, to talk of economies of loss, waste, expenditure and, 'above all', excess.

More specifically, Bataille is referring to what elsewhere he terms the homogeneous and the heterogeneous. The homogeneous, or the sphere dominated by economics, consists of all that is deemed normal, all that seeks to make society a controllable

economy') and what is, strictly speaking, anti-economic, co-exist in the general economy, also means that they interact. The distinction between the two types of economy is never total, even if it is clear cut. This interaction takes a form not dissimilar to Hegel's dialectical system, but with the intervention of Nietzsche – Bataille's system has no overcoming, just the revelation of nothingness, as excess and waste are not recuperable for self-consciousness. We might attempt to incorporate what is threatening to the norms, sanity, life and so on, but such overcoming is already trapped in a restricted economy, rather than the way out of it. For example, taboo and transgression are absolutely linked, as we need a law for there to be a crime, whilst law is the system that believes it has controlled transgression, but no matter how often it enacts this control, the moment of transgression is still beyond it.

Derrida, in 'From Restricted to General Economy' (in *Writing and Difference*), is very interested in Bataille's general economy, acknowledging it as a beyond of Hegel's system – but because of its emphasis on writing, the general economy in Derrida's essay becomes *écriture* (265–7, 273–4). Bataille's text tears itself apart, enacting the violence it describes at a textual level (277), and this, for Derrida, is its lesson – this violence is the process whereby we try and construct meaning and our Being as presence, whilst attacking the possibility of such an event. It is just that Bataille has reversed the process so that the attack becomes primary (this question returns in Chapter 4 below).

Derrida's essay is a perceptive reading of Bataille, and a powerful attack on Sartre, addressing the latter's essay on Bataille, but it does still seek to restrict Bataille – to the realm of language, even if a language now defined by rupture, fragmentation, non-meaning and so on. Indeed for Derrida, because of this we are effectively not to read Bataille at face value, as we are to reject the possibility of Bataille's terms having a content (273). This might seem very sensible when we consider that, as we will see later, Bataille appears to have a belief in a holistic, vitalistic (if nihilistic) model of the universe that uses human sacrifice as its logic, but it is this *sensible* reading that is at issue in Bataille, something to be thrown on the fire. Derrida does go on to say that the terms of the general economy cannot be read as part of a '*system of meaning* permitting or promising an absolute formal mastery'(273), but the net effect of this supposedly careful multiple reading is to erase the threat posed by the content of these terms. Against Derrida then, we should take Bataille at face value, at least initially, and thus not essentially disbelieve him from the start. As it is almost impossible to read Bataille without some suspension of disbelief, we should read Bataille *as if* he were right – an approach that neither believes him nor starts from a critical position.

The problem that lies precisely in (or around) Bataille's writing is its deceptive simplicity, allowing many species of reductionism. The apparent simplicity hides a final indeterminacy, and sometimes difficulties not apparent from superficial readings. In any case, the notion of general economy can be seen, clearly, at first in 'The Notion of Expenditure', and fully in *The Accursed Share*. It is on these two texts that this chapter focuses, via a consideration of the importance of Mauss for Bataille.

The theorization of the general economy is only possible in the light of Mauss's writing on the gift. Bataille accepts the bulk of Mauss's work, *The Gift*, as given, but brings out the more 'metaphysical' aspect, extending the theory in a way that reduces the problems in Mauss, at the same time as it seems to exaggerate them (insofar as Bataille is happy to take all that Mauss says as fact).[2]

Mauss presents analyses of ways of conducting exchange, arguing that the economic as we know it, as something separate from the rest of our social actions, is a historically and geographically

exchange and accumulation, and implicitly challenges the notion that 'primitive' societies live in poverty while we have wealth.[3] What they do have is a different notion of wealth, which emerges from the 'non-economic' exchanges (Mauss argues, nonetheless, that all societies have economies, a market [2]). Mauss writes that forms of exchange that do not involve accumulation can be characterized as 'gift' if they focus on obligations other than possession and to the extent that they are part of a process that remains open. The form that dominates is the potlatch, described as being the 'agonistic type of total prestations' (5). The potlatch involves competition and a series of obligations relating to the gift that draw in a society as whole on the occasion of the exchange.

Potlatch describes the exchanges conducted in Melanesia, and in north-west America. There are three obligations that constitute the potlatch: giving, receiving and returning.[4] One group gives to the other, at a festival-type gathering of the two (the festival itself being part of the potlatch [36–7, 104n.]). The second group is obliged to accept the gift, and in accepting, is also accepting the obligation to return, with interest, what was given. It can be presumed that the first gift was actually already in a chain, and constituted an excessive return of an earlier gift. In many ways, potlatch is characterized by this process of giving against – 'all of the potlatch is in the obligation to return' (*The Gift*, 40, trans. mod.). This is so much the case that the potlatch can consist solely in destruction (35). In some ways, it always is destruction – of value in terms of possession and utility.

The purpose of such exchanges is, initially at least, to be found in the honour that accrues to the 'winner' of the exchange (35), as hierarchy is decided on this basis (72). However, it could be that this is a cultural presumption that relies, precisely where it thinks it does not, on a fixed, universal value, which is actually 'our' way of seeing the results of the potlatch. The potlatch can, alternatively, be seen as an open-ended process, where to win is always transient and which consists of loss and further expenditure (Bataille, *The Accursed Share*, 67; *OC* VII, 70). Mauss's text acknowledges this at other moments, arguing that the gift is in opposition to utilitarianism – i.e. not in the service of a further goal (Mauss, *The Gift*, 69), and that the idea of individual interest is a recent conception (73–4).

ift extended

Given that individual interest does now exist, and that 'modern' societies are engaged in economic systems of production and accumulation, Mauss seeks to show that modern society does not have to be a rapacious money machine: the gift persists in forms such as birthday presents, charity, the interventionist state – all of which are to be encouraged (67). Bataille offers a variant on such a view, but not from the position that there exists such a clear continuity between 'archaic' and 'modern' societies. His position is rather that something like 'the gift', in the form of expenditure (*dépense*) is everywhere, and has to be, or should be, channelled. He arrives at this position, in 'The Notion of Expenditure', after criticizing the concept of utility.

The argument begins with the claim that modern society has reduced humanity to a condition where all values outside of economic ones have been obliterated. He argues that in modern society 'any general judgement of social activity implies the principle that all individual effort, in order to be valid, must be reducible to the fundamental necessities of production and conservation' ('The Notion of Expenditure', 117; *OC* I, 303). The emphasis on utility, on deferred pleasure, 'excludes in principle *nonproductive expenditure*' (ibid.). What is necessary, then, is to rethink such conceptions, as for Bataille the existence of nonproductive expenditure is a given, but it is being constrained. He goes on to outline what he calls, at this point, loss, and its manifestations (in opposition to an economics of gain), in terms of consumption:

> The second part [of consumption] is represented by so-called unpro-
> ductive expenditures: luxury, mourning, war, cults, the erection of

actually made for the phenomena described forming a unity of any sort, but the unity is implicit, and unconcerned with its definitive truthfulness or otherwise. The phenomena of waste or loss are not capable, in a logic of loss, of forming a unity other than heterogeneous. In other words, they have the appearance of belonging together, without for all that forming a coherent whole.

There is no fixed place for any one of the phenomena listed above, although they tend to predominate in 'primitive' societies, and to occur less in 'modern' ones. That said, war makes persistent appearances, and Bataille will vary between accepting it as part of the economy of expenditure, and trying to find ways in which war can be averted (this latter option prevails in *The Accursed Share*). In any case, war is only 'good' if it serves no end but expenditure or future sacrifice (of prisoners). In fact if war is good, then it becomes utilitarian. For Bataille, this is when war is to be criticized. A last point that is made very clearly in the above passage is the differentiation between the consumption proper to consumer society and consumption in the sense of 'consumed in flames'.[5]

The sacred is introduced as being a result of processes of expenditure, as 'from the very first, it appears that sacred things are constituted by an operation of loss' ('The Notion of Expenditure', 119; *OC* I, 306) – i.e. sacrifice. In modern society this subsists in the form of certain elements of art, those that aspire to convey the extremes of existence as expenditure (for the artist and viewer/reader). In this way, poetry features as a form of excess.[6] In addition to this aspect, the possibility of expenditure exists at a social level – and Bataille is not talking about a return to human sacrifice as such.[7] Instead it is the working class who carry this possibility – they are the waste, the loss produced within the system of production.

The bourgeois class does not expend as earlier upper classes did – they spend instead of expend, spend in order to accumulate, and through this accumulation, acquire social power. Such a situation is contrary to that which prevails in societies organized around processes of potlatch, for now expenditure is merely a means to an end, caught within utility ('The Notion of Expenditure', 122–4; *OC* I, 310–13), and in the process a higher level than ever of poverty is created. The miserable condition of the working class becomes the biggest threat to the newly stable productivist realm (this is not to say capitalism is a unified, stable phenomenon, but its participants could be said to be pursuing their own stability, in the form of their profit), and it becomes clear that one economy (the restricted one) actually exists thanks to its expulsion of the other (waste, loss, expenditure) and *that it can now profit from this expulsion*. The economic face of this is, nonetheless, to be seen as part of a restricted economy, along with the imposition of norms, the invention of rules in the religious and judicial realms (themselves also restricted economies), and the pursuit of objective knowledge to add to the stock of truth and knowledge.

To return to the issue of class struggle, the bourgeois class realizes that it has to neutralize the threat posed by its other, the working class, and essentially, its strategy is to invent the interventionist state and incorporate the workers still further (the working class is arguably only ever this incorporation of the lower classes). Bataille is far from defeatist, though, and 'class struggle, on the contrary, becomes the grandest form of social expenditure when it is taken up again and developed, this time on the part of the workers, and on such a scale that it threatens the very existence of the masters' (126; 316).

The prime aim of 'The Notion of Expenditure' is to establish the primacy of loss, waste, expenditure, sacrifice etc. as being more important, more meaningful than accumulation (and less *significant*), under the aegis of the term 'relative utility'. Relative utility is what has been called utility – that which is useful, productive, constructive. Instead of this being the final reason behind any

subsistence or avoid suffering, not because these functions themselves lead to a sufficient result, but in order to accede to the insubordinate function of free expenditure. ('The Notion of Expenditure', 129; *OC* I, 320)[8]

We can also see that the revolution is valorized in its own right, as being 'capable of exerting a force of attraction as strong as the force that directs simple organisms to the Sun' (128; 318). Does this raise a significant problem in the political implications of such a theory? If the Revolution is what is important, why have an idea for what is to follow? Nonetheless, it is clear that the improvement of the existence of the working class is part of Bataille's agenda, and perhaps the question we should be asking is, 'How separate are the domains of utility and loss?', a question that permeates *The Accursed Share*.[9]

Before moving on to that text, it is worth pausing to consider Bataille's style of writing – itself part of this attack on utility. As well as favouring what often can seem pure assertion, he also has a very aggressive and dark style, uncommon in texts of social science, philosophy and the *disciplines* of thought (and if anything the language of 'the human sciences' is even more constricted today, in love with the possibility of its own critical purity). Bataille aims both higher and lower, and 'The Notion of Expenditure' is one of the calmest theoretical essays of this period, and in this essay, in writing of Christianity as a forerunner of the working class revolution, he writes that 'their myths associate social ignominy and the cadaverous degradation of the torture victim with divine splendour', and 'in its immediate form, it wallows in a revolting impurity that is indispensable to its ecstatic torment' (127; 317). What matters that language itself be exceeded, but without neglecting the importance of excessive content (something too readily forgotten by those who would focus on the writing alone).[10] All of which brings us to the hyperbolic intensity of *The Accursed Share*.

The Accursed Share

The notion of expenditure comes to be expressed in more systematic fashion in *The Accursed Share*, a work in which 'the notion of a "general economy" in which the "expenditure" (the "consumption") of wealth, rather than production, was the primary object'(*The Accursed Share*, 9; *OC* VII, 19). If on the one hand, this text serves as the most systematic exposition of Bataille's 'vision', on the other, it most clearly recognizes the paradox thus raised:

> the knowledge acquired was that of an error, an error implied in the coldness that is inherent in all calculation. In other words, my work tended first of all to *increase* the sum of human resources, but its findings showed that this accumulation was only a delay, a shrinking back from the inevitable term, where the accumulated wealth has value only in the instant. (11; 20)

So Bataille has created the same internal relation in his writing that he has with the system of Hegel: the discourse aspiring to truth cannot just be ignored, as this would simply valorize the rejection – make the transgression the law, rather than transgressing the still existing law. Bataille attempts to account for this paradox, implicitly at least, when he clearly states that waste cannot be disentangled from accumulation:

> the notions of 'productive expenditure' and 'nonproductive expenditure' have a basic value in all the developments of my book. But real life, composed of all sorts of expenditures, knows nothing of purely productive expenditure; in actuality, it knows nothing of purely nonproductive expenditure either. (12; 22)

The acknowledgement of this inevitable linkage permeates the book and gives rise to some of its seeming contradictions, as often we are presented with what seems to be a system that is very much one of utility – it has a purpose, it lays out its arguments in

He argues that the economy (in the usual sense) is only one form of processes that are in play, and is essentially the exception to the norm, as everything else is based on waste. He writes that life (including social processes) is a set of manifestations and coalescences of energy, and that this energy serves growth up to a certain point, but then must be expended:

> the excess energy (wealth) can be used for the growth of a system (e.g. an organism); if the system can no longer grow, or if the excess cannot be completely absorbed in its growth, it must necessarily be lost without profit; it must be spent, willingly or not, gloriously or catastrophically. (21; 29)

As it stands, this might seem very close to a system such as Freud's, wherein the organism seeks homeostasis rather than turbulence – once energy is let off, things can go on as they are supposed to – but as we shall see, Bataille's use of the examples of the sun, and of Aztec sacrifice militate against any such easy comparison. In fact as 'energy is always in excess' (23; 31), we can already see that the priority shifts to instability, to expending, as what structures and demands accumulation.

Although Bataille does use the word 'surplus', the continual use of 'excess' renders the sense differently. Excess indicates less a voluntary process and more an uncontrollable element that has to emerge. For Bataille, we have the choice to recognize this, as many societies have, and engage in 'squander' (22; 30) – an active embracing of the principle of excess. Profit (the keeping of what is spare), or the idea of destroying what is merely spare (as in the 'excess capacity' or 'excess production' of manufacturing) should give way to a conception where excess is only excess insofar as it is expended. That is the key difference between profit/surplus and excess: the latter exists only in being expended. If this does not occur, then in some ways 'excess will out', and society will be driven to war to release its energy (23–4; 31–2). At this point Bataille's pseudo-vitalism is proposing that some excesses are better than others and therefore there is a suggestion of health, however perverse, as a result of the 'correct' expenditures. He even puts forward his model as the way of redirecting human activity so that it can avoid war and encourage a more *generous* society:

the extension of economic growth itself requires the overturning of economic principles – the overturning of the ethics that grounds them. Changing from the perspectives of *restricted* economy to those of *general* economy actually accomplishes a Copernican transformation: a reversal of thinking – and of ethics. (25; 33 trans. mod.)

One thing that links Bataille to both Hegel and Nietzsche is the sense that the moment of their idea is indeed the point from which nothing can ever be the same. Furthermore, if some excess is glorious and another catastrophic, then what is at stake here is not at all 'relative' utility, but simply utility – there is no logical reason, at this stage, or at any to come in the argument, why war is not a 'glorious' squander and therefore to be encouraged. Perhaps writing just after the second world war has a bearing on the rejection of a certain ambiguity, shall we say, that was evident in earlier texts, but such squeamishness should not be seen as the necessary reason for him backing down. It would be perfectly possible, in Bataillean terms, to argue that wars divert excess into the profoundest and most noxious *utility*, and that this is the problem with war. Suffice it to say that Bataille does not consistently make such a case.

If all human energy interacts, then so too does all plant and animal life – which also disposes of its own excess (27; 34), but before all this can begin, comes the sun:

solar energy is the source of life's exuberant development. The origin and essence of our wealth are given in the radiation of the sun, which dispenses energy – wealth – without any return. The sun gives without ever receiving. Men were conscious of this long before astrophysics measured that ceaseless prodigality. (28; 35)

In any case, the sun does not gain from the giving, and its giving is a function of waste, of expenditure that founds its reality – the processes which allow the sun a physical, discrete existence are those which expressly oppose such a thing. The solidity of the sun is never present at any one moment. Rather than the existence of planets or life being seen as the gain, the accumulation, that results from the squander of energy on the part of the sun, life is to be seen as a further prodigality – effectively being waste, in the form of 'luxury' (33–5; 40–2). And rather than humanity being the crowning achievement of God, Nature, Evolution, Spirit, Reason, etc. – humanity is the crowning waste – the modernist model of progress is exploded: not only is humanity the biggest waste, but the self-consciousness that is so proud of itself is destined to be and to think its own ruin. Bataille's anti-humanist, but potentially pro-ecologist,[12] position deserves stating at length:

> man is only a roundabout, subsidiary response to the problem of growth. Doubtless, through labour and technique, he has made possible an extension of growth beyond the given limits. But just as the herbivore relative to the plant, and the carnivore relative to the herbivore, is a luxury, man is the most suited of all living beings to consume intensely, sumptuously, the excess energy offered up by the pressure of life to conflagrations befitting the solar origins of its movement. (37; 43)

This is not to just to say that man is good at being wasteful, or that much of what he does recognizes the inherent wastefulness of the universe. Bataille's claim is that all life is luxury – excessive expenditure – and it is such a squander due to the existence of death. Initially, this is far from being a new position – death being a waste, death making any one life a waste or inevitable failure constitutes a very traditional perspective. But Bataille is taking this position to depths unconsidered or rejected by writers such as Hegel, or earlier writers such as Montaigne.

For Bataille, death is not necessary – it represents luxury on the part of nature. He argues that death only comes about late in the history of life, that amoebae, for example, do not have death (32; 39). The increase in complexity of animals, linked with sexual reproduction, both brings death and results from death – in the first case through the death of the individual, and in the second through attempts to circumvent death. As a result of this near-dialectical relation of life and death, 'of all conceivable luxuries, death, in its fatal and inexorable form, is undoubtedly the most costly' (34; 40), as both life and death are inseparable from squander, from the expenditure of excess energy in nature. Human existence manages to extend this wastefulness through its labour, its *arts*, and the creation of a position where there is a gap between the individual, the world and the population as a whole – a gap which is at the root of the belief in accumulation: 'as a rule, *particular* existence always risks succumbing for lack of resources. It contrasts with *general* existence whose resources are in excess and for which death has no meaning' (39; 45).

As our 'modern' societies have forgotten the principle of expending without need for return, and the need for loss has not gone away in the now generalized (but not *general*) economy, Bataille now reintroduces the question of what the possibilities are for our society if we follow his thesis. He does not propose a return to human sacrifice (although the reporting of wars and 'tragedies' perhaps comes to fill some of the vacuum). Essentially, all that he proposes is redistribution, as Mauss did before him, and he has the grace to be somewhat embarrassed that this is the answer ('it seems rather disappointing to have nothing more to propose, as a remedy for the catastrophe that threatens, than the "raising of the living standard"' [41; 47]). He argues that, in terms of the general economy, it is not about ensuring an equal or even equitable standard of living, but about removing the occasion for unacceptable excess in the form of war and discontent leading to riots and so on

sections Bataille traces the progressive decline of expenditure, sacrifice and economies of loss, via the Aztecs, Islam, Lamaism, early and contemporary capitalism (with reference to Tawney and Weber on Protestantism). As historical data, however, they are less than satisfactory, often ending in huge generalizations that seem inconsistent with arguments made elsewhere. Just because Bataille might desire a 'heterogeneous' way of writing, arguing etc., this does not mean that when he is claiming to cite facts he can say what he likes (the section on Islam is particularly weak). Perhaps it would be better to see the later sections of the book as illustrations of the theory – in fact, the section on Aztec sacrifice is vital to the argument of the 'theoretical' section, as are the theoretical points about utility raised once more in the sections on capitalist society.

Bataille argues that humanity has lost the sacred, has lost something he calls 'intimacy' (57; 62), which is a relation of immediacy with everything (a shift valorized by Hegel throughout *Phenomenology*, as the development of self-consciousness), and this came about as a result of labour – the clear distinction between worker and what is worked:

> the first labour established the world of *things*, to which the profane world of the Ancients generally corresponds. Once the world of things was posited, man himself became one of the things of the world, at least for the time in which he laboured. It is this degradation that man has always tried to escape. In his strange myths, in his cruel rites, man is *in search of a lost intimacy* from the first. (*The Accursed Share*, 57; *OC* VII, 62)

In this formulation we see the paradoxical coming together of the supposed opposites of Sade and Rousseau – Rousseau's valorizing of a nature that is always lost, and Sade's violent response to the absence of truth in Nature, God, Humanity. The Aztecs (and any peoples engaged in human sacrifice) had a response to this situation – with the time of sacrifice being the space of irruption of the sacred, the realm of death, loss, waste and expenditure. This is because 'sacrifice restores to the sacred world that which servile use has degraded, rendered profane' (55; 61), and the sacrificed must represent something worth sacrificing. As kings got weary of themselves being worth sacrificing, new categories of worthy victims would be introduced (warriors, virgins etc., or even someone who would be a prince for a set period, and then sacrificed). Victims must be deemed worth sacrificing, and are worth sacrificing insofar as they represent a sacrificing of worth:

> the victim is a surplus taken from the mass of *useful* wealth. And he is only withdrawn from it in order to be consumed profitlessly, and therefore utterly destroyed. Once chosen, he is the *accursed share*, destined for violent consumption. But the curse tears him away from the *order of things*. (59; 64)

The 'accursed share' *is* that which is 'destined for consumption', i.e. that which must be sacrificed, that which is the excess of society. Surely it is perverse to say that certain people must be killed for society to get on in a way that acknowledges excess in an acceptable way, but the accursed share can in theory be anything – it could be the element of the harvest destined for the gods, for example. Bataille does argue that only a society that really values people sacrifices them – the substitution of animals for humans simply illustrates the progressive 'thingness' of humanity, as fairly soon even this is deemed too much and the substitution becomes symbolic, in the feeble sense (i.e. signifying) of the word.[14]

A further complaint could be that sacrifice is just a way of controlling the people – whether through the direct sacrifice of troublemakers, or through fear and respect. The Aztecs, after all, were a conquering society. Such an argument is a strong imputation of utility and a functionalist, carceral model of society, which really only belongs to modern Europe. Even if the argument is

of sacrificer, sacrificed and participants (the category of observer being logically excluded as it presumes an objective distance) is dissolved as it is instituted (at the moment of sacrifice). According to Bataille, this all comes together in the sun: 'the sun himself was in their eyes the expression of sacrifice' (46; 52), and war was necessary not in order to gain territory but to shed blood, both in fighting and in sacrifice. Most importantly, 'the Mexicans thought that if they ceased [war and sacrifice] the sun would cease to give light' (49; 55).

This last point, in its way, is the most logical reason for sacrifice – and this is the problem – it is a *reason* for sacrifice, it has utility, despite its seeming arbitrariness. Bataille seems totally unaware that here the general economy is undermined and incapable of seeing that 'general utility' as opposed to 'relative utility' allows that what Bataille sees as helpful in opening the way to purposeless loss is in fact another way of conceiving utility, which only *looks* different because Bataille too is trapped within a limited, Western concept of utility.[16]

Following his discussion of Aztec sacrifice, Bataille moves on to the potlatch, at which point it becomes clear that all of what has preceded this section in some way flows from it: the sun's gift, the return of the Aztecs, the receipt of the gift in life in between. At one level the potlatch is another recognition of the senseless waste of the universe, and at another, the senseless waste of the universe is Bataille's rendering of the potlatch as universal. But if we regard these sections, on societies based on *consumation*, as being extensions of the theory, rather than evidence of its veracity, it begins to fit together more 'acceptably'.

Bataille's reading of Mauss privileges the destructive side of 'the potlatch' but, like Mauss, he draws no distinction between giving and destroying (within the potlatch), noting that as well as the expenditure of sacrifice as such, the Aztecs held festivals of great expense. The paradoxical economy that emerges from these practices of loss he identifies as the 'general economy' (68; 71). In the theorization he offers, it is clear that the side of accumulation is not simply to be left out – he is not proposing a simple opposition of expenditure and appropriation, even if on many occasions this split does seem to be apparent. What he proposes is a model that unites both types of what are now to be recognized as economical phenomena so that their interaction can be identified, and this interaction defined by waste, squander, loss etc. – as all accumulation is itself to be thought of as wasteful.

Bataille recognizes that much of the activity identified in terms of loss, or in terms of the potlatch, is explicitly destined to increase the status of the 'winner', even if this winner only wins through losing. This does not preclude the fact that this win is predicated on loss, and at the moment of exchange is loss. Bataille moves on from Mauss's position to make this loss something overtly metaphysical, in the sense that we are not talking about material gains and losses alone.[17] The following passage throws up all the complexity of Bataille's position, and the inherent *obligation* that underlies the obligation within the exchange itself:

> we need on the one hand to go beyond the narrow limits within which we ordinarily remain, and on the other hand somehow bring our going-beyond back within our limits. [. . .] Gift-giving has the virtue of a surpassing of the subject who gives, but in exchange for the object given, the subject appropriates the surpassing: he regards his virtue, that which he had a capacity for, as an asset, as a *power* that he now possesses. (69; 72)

This going-beyond is specifically not transcendence, but the exceeding of the subject in exchange. The subject, who loses himself (e.g. in participating in the festival of sacrifice) tries to control this, to master this outside encountered in gift-giving. The prime means of doing this is to view it as a gain, as something achieved, or as something known. In other words, any power that emerges from sacrif can no longer control its processes of acquisition. Convenient though it would be to leave it there, one of the most puzzling aspects of *The Accursed Share* remains: the recommendations and observations on postwar politics.

Bataille regards the Marshall Plan as an exemplary form of the general economy, in that it constitutes a gift that emerges from the excess of the United States' production, whilst at the same time this gift is expected to be compensated for by the renewed capacity of those who are assisted to spend. Bataille does not mention the further parallel with the potlatch of the obligation to repay. Many countries in today's economy (restricted sense) are under a burden to repay several times over what they borrowed.

The Marshall Plan, then, serves to bring nonproductive expenditure in, in a way that seems acceptable to societies dominated by a 'Protestant ethic' of utility and acquisition (182; 172). Such societies do know sumptuary expenditure in, for example, spectacles or sporting events, but these are not enough to prevent the outpouring of war that may result from imbalances at a worldwide level. In the closing section of the book, on the Marshall Plan, Bataille is near to Freudian models of homeopathic outbursts (expending to create absence of stimuli) in order to maintain a general tranquillity – in other words, utility and all associated concepts are in play, when it comes to the practical level of 'what is to be done'.

Similarly, in his account of 'Soviet industrialization', Bataille valorizes what we would not expect – this very industrialization which seems the apotheosis of thingness he has earlier attacked. The principal reason for this peculiar take is that bourgeois existence is the realm of things and pretends it is not, as individualism both relies on things, and makes the person a more discrete entity and therefore more separated off than ever before (138; 132). Communism, even in its Stalinist form, does not pretend to such freedom, and specifically attacks the bourgeois individual. For Bataille, 'the modern bourgeois appears as the poorest figure of a person that humanity has assumed, but to this "person" inured to the isolation and mediocrity of his life, communism offers a death leap' (150; 141–2). The Stalinist Soviet Union is not being praised in an unqualified manner by Bataille, and its crucial role is perhaps to be seen in the way it forces the West to adapt: the threat of atomic war and of internal revolutions forces the West to temper its accumulative drive.

Just as he is turning into an advocate of an arch pragmatism, Bataille shifts once more to a consideration of the role of 'sovereignty' in thought and how this permeates actions in a general economy that recognizes waste, loss, excess (189–90; 177–9). This sudden turn, emerging from practical considerations, is a typical shift. The way in which Bataille has sought to bring everything into this concept of general economy, at every stage, while leaving it totally porous, is as important as what he says about the general economy as such, because it filters into all the main works, and can serve as a means of organizing our thought of Bataille. In this way, the general economy is a conception of the economic that leaves 'the economy' behind; it is the reality of the writing of *The Accursed Share*, and finally, it is the perpetually disappearing wholeness in Bataille's work, such that what he writes does not develop, nor does it build. Instead the same thing is written, over and over, different every time, with itself as object, as well as the objects it ostensibly addresses, and the objects it seeks to destroy.

Notes

1. For a detailed critique of the belief in the universality of production and something like 'the economic', which effectively is building on Bataille's work, see Baudrillard, *The Mirror of Production*.

2. Evans-Pritchard argues that the relevance of this ~~essay~~ ~~~~

~~the empirical~~ ~~~~

52   *Georges Bataille*

Stone Age Economics and Baudrillard argues that the notion of subsistence is moral rather than economic (*The Mirror of Production*, 81–2).

4. See 'The Three Obligations: Giving, Receiving, Repaying' (*The Gift*, 37–41). The title of this section is noteworthy for how it economizes the original. 'Rendre' is not necessarily as financial as repaying. There are many problems with the translation of *The Gift*, and many of them, perhaps instructively, consist of just such a reincorporation of key terms into a narrower sense of economics.

5. In French, the distinction can be made between *consommation* for the first, and *consumation* for the second. *Consumation* was to have been the title of the first part of *The Accursed Share*. It retains this as a subtitle in *OC* VII. Further material on the question of expenditure exists in this volume, under the title of *La Limite de l'utile* ('The Limit of the Useful'), 181–280.

6. See also *The Impossible* (*OC* III, 97–223). This was originally titled 'The Hatred of Poetry'. The closing section (157–64; 217–23) argues that 'true poetry is outside laws' (158; 218), and that 'poetry which does not raise itself to the nonsense of poetry is only the emptiness of poetry, merely lovely poetry' (*OC* III, 220.). Bataille's own overtly poetic writings, many of which appear in *OC* III, IV and V do not, for all of this, attack language at a formal level to any great extent. For what is in a way a more complete Bataillean shift from death and waste into the excess of poetry, see Baudrillard, *Symbolic Exchange and Death*.

7. In '[Note sur le système actuel de répression]' ('Note on the Present System of Repression'), *OC* II, 134–6, he argues that as it is impossible to return to the days of glorious and bloody expenditure, all reasons for killing and stealing should be removed – i.e. property is to be abolished (134).

8. On the question of relative utility, see also '[Le paradoxe de l'utilité absolue]' ('The Paradox of Absolute Utility'), *OC* II, 147–52. In this text, Bataille is posing the questions he begins to respond to in 'The Notion of Expenditure'.

9. Bataille accuses Stalin of helping to prevent world revolution, as envisaged by Lenin and Trotsky, through his implementation of 'socialism in one country' (*The Accursed Share*, 149; *OC* VII, 141). See also 'Les guerres sont pour le moment les plus forts stimulants de l'imagination' ('Wars Are at This Time the Strongest Stimulants for the Imagination') (*OC* II, 392–9). In this essay Bataille addresses the question of the issue of revolution, and here at least, the question of revolution is answered in a way that suggests Bakunin rather than Marx. Bataille argues that whilst war is only (a) good if and when it is won and that revolution is an end in itself – with value beyond that of its use as a means to an end (393–4). This does not exclude the fact that even this expenditure is conducted in the name of a future gain: 'there are no wars, revolutions or religious movements that do not promise a gain in exchange for the total giving of self [don de soi sans réserves] they demand' (393). This *promise* could itself be seen as partaking in an economy of excess, and is never exactly the same as 'its' realization.

10. The reading of Bataille for his contribution to *écriture* parallels the reading made of Sade by the surrealists, who disgusted Bataille with their way of reducing Sade to being a therapist/liberationist of general desire, rather than providing a threat to all law, whilst insisting on the inevitability of law and guilt (see 'The Use

Value of D.A.F. de Sade', in particular, and also 'Dossier de la polémique avec André Breton', (*OC* II, 51–109)).

11. Elsewhere Bataille draws attention to the possibility that what he was doing was phenomenology and uses the opportunity to point to the deficiency in Hegel's approach: 'Hegelian phenomenology represents the mind as essentially homogeneous' ('Attraction and Repulsion II: Social Structure', 117; *OC* II, 320), and therefore the various elements of heterogeneity constitute ' a notion that is entirely foreign to Hegel' (117; 321). With regard to the position of the sun in Bataille's thought, Derrida has commented on Bataille's use of 'the sun' as being the centre of his system ('Economimesis'). Similar arguments have been put forward by writers such as Geoff Bennington ('Introduction to Economics I: Because the World is Round'), and Rodolphe Gasché, in *The Tain of the Mirror: Derrida and the Philosophy of Reflection*.

12. His position signals developments that will come under the banner of 'deep ecology', which is highly critical of other ecologisms, as trying to ensure the prolongation of the current ecosystem, within which humanity is top of the chain/pile. Accordingly, a true ecology does not care whether humanity survives: there will always be an ecology, if not this one. See Arne Naess, *Ecology, Community and Lifestyle*, for a statement of this philosophy, and Murray Bookchin et al., *Deep Ecology and Anarchism*, for a range of critiques.

13. Bataille has earlier drawn the distinction between what is acceptable and what is useful. As there is always going to be loss, 'it is only a matter of an acceptable loss, preferable to another that is regarded as unacceptable: a question of *acceptability*, not utility. Its consequences are decisive, however' (*The Accursed Share*, 31; *OC* VII, 37). What seems at the outset a very apt distinction is turned, at the end, into something that aims for a goal other than itself, and is therefore perhaps not utility in the sense of being directly useful in an accumulation, or growth, but is still something very close to a concept of the useful.

14. In later texts (*Lascaux, The Tears of Eros*), Bataille argues the opposite, claiming that animal sacrifice came first, but then, as we lost our sense of community with animals, we lost our sense that something of the highest value was being sacrificed. The only thing that could have such a value was a human

sun as the origin of everything, and the sun might as well stand for knowledge, truth, self-present Being, due to its singularity. On the issue of 'use value' in Bataille, see Hollier, 'The Use-Value of the Impossible'. This essay subtly counters those who seek to find new use values in Bataille, in arguing that through Bataille we can reconceive use value as being an impossible moment, rather than something to be restored. For Hollier, Bataille attacks the 'longing for a world subject to the tyranny of use-value' (138).

17. According to Baudrillard, Bataille has ' "naturalised" Mauss, but in a meta-physical spiral so prodigious that the reproach is not really one' ('When Bataille Attacked the Metaphysical Principle of Economy', 61). So the move to render more metaphysical is in fact what undoes the unstated metaphysic of Mauss's argument (that humanity is generous), in that it makes this *excessive*, uncontrollable and vio-lent. A further point to be noted about Baudrillard's reading of 'the gift' is that Mauss is to be read against himself, through Bataille, such that the counter-gift pre-dominates. In other words, the process of violent gift-giving dominates, in light of the fact that a gift is always already a counter-gift, once we are in Bataille's solar system (Baudrillard, *Symbolic Exchange and Death*, 2 and *passim*).

3

Death

Death is a continual concern for Bataille, from the earliest writings, to the last fizzles in and around *The Tears of Eros*, and arguably sits at the centre of the general economy, as death can be seen as 'the ultimate term of possible expenditure' ('Attraction and Repulsion II', 123; *OC* II, 332 trans. mod.). Bataille's notion of death is an empty version of Hegel's: it is negativity, but one that cannot be recuperated, even if all our actions can be seen as attempts at such a recuperation. Death is the loss that defines our existence as individuals, since sexual reproduction is absolutely caught up with the death of the individual; unlike amoebae, there is no continuity of Being from one organism to the next (*The Accursed Share*, 32; *OC* VII, 39. See also *Eroticism*, 12–15; *OC* X. 17–21). Death

always be possible to show that whichever primordial fact gets priority presupposes the existence of another one' (*The Accursed Share*, vol. II, 82; *OC* VIII, 71).[1]

Death features in early writings – 'beings only die to be born', 'Solar Anus', 7; *OC* I, 84), and becomes something that does not transcend the individual so much as lose the individual in a generalized excess. Instead of Hegel's mastery of death, we see that

> in the fact that life and death are passionately devoted to the subsidence of the void, the relation of master/slave subordination is no longer revealed, but life and void are confused and mingled like lovers, in the convulsive moments of the end. ('Sacrifices', 133; *OC* I, 93 trans. mod.)

Instead of giving in to death, accepting it at a distance, as the distancing that structures Being (Heidegger), death is to be embraced, as 'it appears that no less a loss than death is needed for the brilliance of life to traverse and transfigure dull existence' ('The Practice of Joy Before Death', 239; *OC* I, 557). This is not because death is so marvellous, but because it is everywhere, linking the individual to everything else (what Bataille will go on to call the general economy):

> I can only perceive a succession of cruel splendours whose very movement requires that I die: this death is only the *exploding* consumption of all that was, the joy of existence of all that comes into the world; even my own life demands that everything that exists, everywhere, ceaselessly give itself and be annihilated. ('The Practice of Joy Before Death', 239; *OC* I, 557)

Bataille is not arguing from the perspective whereby the universe only exists in one's own mind, but that even we, pathetic individuals that we are, feature in the ceaseless process of death and destruction. This linkage of the individual, through death, to others, to the general economy, is what is pursued in Bataille's connecting of the erotic with death, which is a development of the linkage between sex and death. In *Eroticism* he uses the term 'continuity' to designate both the state of shared existence of asexual reproduction and what lies beyond individuality when individuals lose themselves in sacrifice, erotic activity, laughter, drunkenness and so on (*Eroticism*, 11–25; *OC* X, 17–30). These attempts interest him because 'eroticism opens the way to death. Death opens the way to the denial of our individual selves' (24; 29).

The second volume of *The Accursed Share*, subtitled *The History of Eroticism*, is often seen as being little more than a draft version of *Eroticism*, but there are crucial differences in emphasis. *The History of Eroticism* really is a genuine part of the work on 'the accursed share', whereas such an economy is only implicit in *Eroticism*. More importantly still, the former seeks to link sexuality to death, and the latter attempts the opposite movement (both movements, for no clear theoretically necessary reason, lead Bataille to associate 'Woman' with death). The second volume of *The Accursed Share* even starts by stating that it is not really about eroticism, but is instead 'a thinking that does not fall apart in the face of horror', emerging from 'a *system* of thought exhausting the totality of the possible' (*The Accursed Share*, vol. II, 14; *OC* VIII, 10). In writing about death as part of the general economy, it also emerges that death is not necessarily literal death. But we should on no account take it as simply a metaphor, as metaphors imply a reality to be represented, and Bataille offers no such real world, existing to be represented in mimesis, metaphor or metonymy.

Death and Fear

Hegel sees death as the origin of humanity's self-consciousness (this being, initially, consciousness of death), and the rest of time consists of the struggle to master death. Communal existence is also centred around death, and the two combine in the form of

At the same time as humanity is drawn toward death, it pushes it away – this repulsion is what defines humanity. Repulsion is the key word, as death is not simply a negativity, something that happens to the subject, but something that, even when it happens to someone else, provokes disgust. Humanity is defined by its 'repugnance for death' (*The Accursed Share*, vol. II, 61; *OC* VIII, 51). This is hardly a novel or shocking statement, but death is specifically part of what repels us because we repel it, and arguably the (primordial) object of disgust (and only in becoming human does death constitute something disgusting). Humans have a horror of all that threatens their unitary existence: excretions, filth, loss of control through drunkenness, eroticism (61–2; 51–2). More than this, we also have a horror of life, as at some level we are aware of life as a by-product of death, so much so that 'we might think, if need be, that living matter *on the very level we separate ourselves from it* is the privileged object of our disgust' (63; 52). All such disgusts are caught up within taboos, in a relation where it is impossible to ascertain whether the taboo created the disgust, or responds to it. For Bataille, however, death really is at the heart of the existence of taboo, but is not the exclusive centre:

> since it goes without saying, I will not linger over the possible anteriority of the horror of death. This horror is perhaps at the root of our repugnance (the loathing of nothingness would then be at the origin of the loathing of decay, which is not physical since it is not shared by animals). It is clear, in any event, that the nature of excrement is analogous to that of corpses and that the places of its emission are close to the sexual parts; more often than not, this complex of prohibitions appears inextricable. (79; 68)

This complex marks the line of demarcation between human and other and proximity to these phenomena constitutes *the crossing of this line*. This crossing and the fear of crossing gives the 'universally human character of the problem of obscenity' (54; 45), even if *contra* Freud and Lévi-Strauss, for example, there is no particular taboo that is universal.[3] Death is also 'at the beginning' insofar as its appearance coincides with labour and utility – this is what makes death a problem for the individual, as the individual conceives of his or her self as something to be maintained, preserved and developed (82; 70).[4]

Death very rapidly becomes the site of prohibition, and takes two principal forms: both murder and 'contact with corpses' are forbidden (79; 68). It is not the metaphysical difficulty of impending death that creates this fear, since this arises from an awareness that life is an accident between waste and decay, with only waste and decay in between. As Bataille notes, 'life is a luxury of which death is the highest degree' (85–6; 74) and 'moreover, life is a product of putrefaction' (80; 69), so death and decay are linked to conceptions of our birth and origin (for him, this accounts for 'our' fear of menstrual blood, for example). Here, as elsewhere, it is striking how far Bataille goes down a road attacking preconceptions only to launch into a restatement of tired clichés about 'woman' as other, as death. He simply does not question the taboos around 'woman', and this is why Kristeva's gloss on Bataille (*Powers of Horror*) and Mary Douglas's *Purity and Danger* is so successful – it completes the logic already under way.

The all-pervasive absence, or denial, of death, through prohibition, is why death is to be approached, and also why we have an attraction to as well as repulsion from death and all that threatens our identity, so that for example, 'eroticism, it may be said, is assenting to life up to the point of death' (*Eroticism*, 11; *OC* X, 17). Death and eroticism remain charged with danger, and create anguish in individuals as their individuality falls away (*The Accursed Share*, vol. II, 101; *OC* VIII, 88).[5] But as with Hegel's 'facing up to death', Bataille does not limit the notion of death to actual biological death – it comes to include all that undoes the individual, such

awareness of an impossibility (we do not even *gain* nothing, as asceticism would aspire to), but what will have happened is the following:

> the embrace restores us, not to nature (which is itself, if it is not rein-tegrated, only a detached part), but rather to the totality in which man has his share by *losing himself.* For an embrace is not just a fall into the animal muck, but the anticipation of death, and the putrefaction that fol-lows it. (119; 103)

There is no why, however, and there can only be 'virtual' replies to 'why?' – i.e. there can be the project of approaching death, as it enhances subjectivity, but this project is lost at the moment it is attained, whether in actual death or in death-like experience (non-experience). Note also that the only 'return' is to something that is necessarily lost, again and again. Eroticism, then, is one direction waste or excess can take that involves death (itself waste, excess), but Bataille also hints at another level at which death can be approached – a level that really is metaphorical.

He argues that fiction, if written intensely, can stimulate the anguish and loss of self that other actions can induce directly, with the difference that 'an object fascinates in sacrifice – or in lit-erature – which is not ordinarily present in horror or anguish' (107; 92). In other words, we are attracted to something, as well as horrified by it, whereas outside of these settings it would simply horrify us. In fact at this point Bataille seems to be sug-gesting that literature and art are the only ways we can actually approach that which is 'outside'; he goes on to state that 'we want to be intoxicated with vertigo, and the image of the fall suffices for this' (109; 94). The last thing we want is to really die – as this would end all further encounters with death, loss, luxury, and so on. Whilst this last aspect is a partial justification for what is in effect a fairly thin model of catharsis, the question remains as to how far something like art, with its inevitable distance from viewer, reader or listener, can induce effects of loss of self. If any-thing, maybe Bataille could be taken as saying that what we want might be to control death or 'the other' through powerful art, but in actual fact, death will always elude us, and then occur, dis-sipating us. What can never occur is that will and consciousness subsist at the point of 'intensity'.

Abjection

The passage of death and revulsion of death into its substitutes or surrogates (in art, sacrifice, eroticism) does not always occur, and must in any case be 'continually enforced'. Once again, there are hints at a Freudian economy of homeostasis, but a detailed consideration of this *passage* shows that while it is not incompatible with psychoanalysis, it is something beyond Freud.[6] The particular idea that stands for this transitional state of horror (one which can become permanent) is abjection. The most well known exponent of a theory of abjection is Julia Kristeva, in her *Powers of Horror*, but essentially the theory is already there in Bataille, in a way that eludes psychoanalysis (and in fact Kristeva's book often pushes against the limits of psychoanalysis). For Kristeva, the notion of abjection is all about transition, liminality (crossing borders of subject and object), and enforced transition. For Bataille, it could be that life is just such a transition.

The key essay is 'L'abjection et les formes misérables' (*OC* II, 217–21), but the term features elsewhere in Bataille, and the concept is certainly present at many points.[7] One of its later appearances indicates that all life could be seen as a premonition of abjection; Bataille writes that 'I will rejoin abject nature and the purulence of anonymous, infinite life, which stretches forth like the night, which is death. One day this living world will pullulate in my dead mouth' (*The Accursed Share*, vol. II, 81; *OC* VIII, 70).

Bataille is often seen as valorizing states that others regard as

Bataille is totally opposed to Freud's models of curing or mediating neurosis – there can be no final exclusion that does not in turn create an excluded that will resurface. Abjection is the term Bataille uses to denote this double movement of exclusion and intrusion.

The corpse is at the start of abjection as a fearful relation to otherness but, logically speaking, it is perhaps abjection that makes the corpse seem threatening, as 'the exclusion of what is rotten is constitutive of man, and understanding this must be taken as the base for the understanding of man himself' (*OC* II, 439n.). The corpse, then, could be seen as the focusing device, rendering a formless horror certain – as recognition of the putative and inevitable loss of self arises. But we can go further back, and find the origin of abjection to be always lost. Abjection 'has an absence as its origin: it is simply the inability to assure with enough force the necessary act of excluding abject things ([an act] which constitutes the foundation of collective existence)' (*OC* II, 219). This absence is to be read two ways: firstly, that there is no set origin for it; secondly, it is the absence that creates abjection (such as the absence of life in the corpse).

The notion of abjection surfaces in other early essays, and if we were to include all the times Bataille writes about what has been marginalized as disgusting the list would never end, but there are certain key references. In 'The Use Value of D.A.F. de Sade', mention is made of a '*corps étranger*' (foreign body) (92, 94, 101; *OC* II, 56, 58, 68), as that which the body seeks to control and excrete – ensuring its distancing through temporary ingestion (his example is the coprophagy in *The 120 Days of Sodom*).[8] Elsewhere, abjection is mentioned in the context of 'attraction and repulsion', and this leads into the consideration of how abjection takes on a properly social character.[9]

In 'Abjection', Bataille argues that abjection does not exist only for the individual, but that it has a social dimension, resulting from class exploitation. He argues that the wretched condition the lower classes find themselves in is a result of their deprivation (as Engels had also argued, in *The Condition of the Working Class in England*). This abjection, however, is not something that can simply be solved by reorganizing society, as the terrible condition of the working class (and their exclusion) is self-perpetuating (*OC* II, 219). So, the middle class excludes its repulsive other, the working class, but the working class is unable to expel its misery, and therefore it remains abject. In one sense Bataille is outlining a nineteenth-century vision here, but in another, we could look at the way in which today working-class culture is vilified (or at how an under-class, or non-working class is vilified by the self-righteous working class), and argue that the process of exclusion and repulsion is still active.

From this point, Bataille has a tendency to link the classes excluded by capitalist society to phenomena such as eroticism and sacrifice, as things that resist the mundanity, the utility of the homogeneous bourgeois world, but what he does not do is recommend a willing embrace of awful conditions – what is abject *is* fearful, nasty, dangerous and so on, and has its own perverse attraction, but not because what was low is now to be thought of as high (acceptable, right, proper).

Existence should, for Bataille, consist of expulsion of what is abject, on a regular basis, via a certain approaching. For example, he argues that 'primitive societies' do not have the abject, as they are able to exclude it through their rituals (*OC* II, 437n.). This seems a contradiction, for surely it is the 'primitive' society that has more of a relation to the abject: it does not, for example, hide its dead away in the way we do. Bataille appears to be arguing that they are in fact repelling the abject on a more continuous basis than 'modern' society – or is it that the latter is truly abject? Perhaps we can say that 'primitive' societies have abjection as a process, rather than being in abjection, as their condition.

Abjection, then, emerges from the horror of the repulsed, while also causing this horror at some indefinable moment, a moment that then spreads out and encompasses all the margins of both the individual and society, so that it resembles closely the excess of the general economy. Such a moment of gathering occurs in the following fragment:

In practice, the expelled human life consisting of the excess, itevels life, abject elements, even when denied, have the determining role in erotic attraction, and from this example, we can see that the value of such elements rests on the always latent possibility, that of the transformation of repulsion into attraction. ('En effet la vie humaine . . .' [In Practice, Human Life . . .'], *OC* II, 163)

Death and the Feminine

It has almost become a truism, in what is called 'French feminism', that 'masculine' philosophy centres on death, and seeks to embrace death instead of life and birth.[11] As Annie Leclerc, in *Parole de femme*, notes, 'Death. Death. Death . . . For if desire is the only thing on their lips, their hearts harbour only dreams of death' (77). On the basis of Bataille's conception of death, he certainly seems to be engaging in a profoundly masculine project, which would reinscribe mastery where it supposedly loses it. Now, if Bataille gets beyond the phenomenological idea of overcoming, or living through death, he is arguably still within the orbit of a desire to control, insofar as woman comes to stand as part of the other for man. If she is a site that can be known, despite being other, and she features as a form of death, then all Bataille's attempts *not* to flee or to know death will fail.

Throughout *Powers of Horror*, Kristeva insists on the link between the abject and the maternal *for the male*, even if logically there is no reason for women not to be part of abjection in the same way.[12] The linkage receives its most forceful formulation when Kristeva ostensibly discusses abjection in the context of the Old Testament: 'mother and death, both abominated, abjected, slyly build a victimising and persecuting machine at the cost of which I become subject of the Symbolic as the Other of the Abject' (112 trans. mod.). Instead of the mother being part of birth and creation, male 'creativity' relies on the mother becoming an instrument of death or castration, while at the same time *her* subjectivity is removed. As the other of Man, Woman occupies the non-place of death, and death is the domain of Man. Margaret Whitford, writing on Irigaray, argues that for the latter, 'woman is used by the male imaginary to deflect or mediate the death drives of *men* [. . .], there are no social/symbolic forms which mediate *their* death' (*The Irigaray Reader*, 159).[13] Death is the preserve of men, and that preserve is Woman. For Hélène Cixous, Bataille takes Hegel a long way from his portentous view of death, but is not totally removed from 'the (Hegelian) schema of recognition, [where] there is no place for the other, for an equal other, for a whole and living woman' ('Sorties', *The Newly Born Woman*, 79).

There is another, more superficial level at which the issue of death becomes a problem for feminism, this time of another, more traditional variety, and that is the question of violence against women in the form of pornography. Andrea Dworkin is forceful in her attack on Bataille, among many others, for contributing to a culture of violence against women. As Suleiman and Still have both pointed out, Dworkin has missed the subtlety of Bataille's fictions, and replaced it with her own, more pornographic version.[14] In any case, we need to consider whether this question is related to the other, 'deeper' question about masculine metaphysics. For Dworkin, it is not just Bataille who is to blame, but his readers, who are complicit in his construction of 'a meaning of sex which is death' (*Pornography*, 175). Furthermore, this real meaning sex is supposed to have for the male writer, and those complicit with him, leads to several forms of annihilation for the woman: 'in some cases, the death is literal. In some cases, it is the annihilation of female will' (176). For this to be the case in Bataille's fiction requires a very selective reading, as often it is the male narrator who suffers, and who is *barely present* in the text. In addition, Bataille's theoretical writing could be advanced as support for the contention that everyone should behave excessively, lose control,

within this economy. Woman, for Bataille, tends to be the place where birth and death combine – both being limit experiences for a human individual, and both having to do with the erotic. According to Still, 'the anguished juxtaposition and attempted fusion of seemingly distinct entities [. . .] evokes on some level what are problems for us all: sexual difference, loss of meaning, death' ('Horror in Kristeva and Bataille', 233), but notwithstanding this, there are moments (in Bataille's theory) when the death of the 'I' seems predicated on a sexual difference wherein the male starts from the position of subject, whilst the female always occupies the position of object. In much of Bataille's fiction this is not the case, in that the protagonists are often women, without having to stand for 'Woman', and seem to have at least as much possibility of losing their *subjecthood* in excess as the male characters.

Women, then, seem to be privileged with regard to access to the realm of the erotic, or death. Significantly, Bataille writes that women are to be found at the 'centre of eroticism' in a way that men are not (*The Accursed Share*, vol. II, 436n.; *OC* VIII, 103n.). They also have a more proximate relation to birth and death, as a result of this, which means that if 'life is a product of putrefaction' (80; 69), then women are *within* such an abjection. Women also constitute a particular form of object for the (male) subject: 'a naked woman, young and pretty, is doubtless the exemplary form of the object' (137; 110). Bataille specifies that women are *regarded* as objects (139; 120–1), but this does not prevent him accepting that this being regarded as 'object' effectively entails being the object. Combining this statement of women as object with their status within death/eroticism etc., means they are specifically not objects, but constitute the 'male abject'. Woman 'opens onto death' (153; 132) through her beauty, which brings on the 'little death'. In *Madame Edwarda* her cunt is 'the bared wound' (150; *OC* III, 21 trans. mod.).[16] In *La Tombe de Louis XXX*, the narrator opens 'your' legs 'like a book where I read what kills me' (*OC* IV, 161). In notes to 'Le Mort', woman is 'the mask of death' (*OC* IV, 366n.).

My Mother brings many of these issues together. The sun, death, the narrator's mother, God – all come together (50; *OC* IV, 203). The mother declares that she wanted to bring her son into the world of death and corruption, and 'I wanted to lead you into my death' (133; 276). In *My Mother*, she is all – subject and what lies outside the subject. The son is nothing. So at one level it is a woman who is central here as agent and as death/object, but at another level is she not, when *written* into subjecthood, just the crowning moment of masculine sublimation, a way of controlling fears about death/castration? This would be a comical way of reading Bataille, even if in some way it seems to be akin to what he believes. The last thing Bataille can be accused of is having an unconscious – all is on the surface. Could this not be the sublimation, however? In that case, we would have to ask why the balance between horror, death and sex never moves to resolution – there is no mastery of the situation, for male or female actors in the fictions. If for a moment we attribute some validity to the claims of psychoanalysis, we would still have to recognize that psychoanalysis is the limited, restricted economy to Bataille's general economy of sex and death: it is psychoanalysis that is the sublimation, the defence mechanism, built on the belief in solid identity (for male subjects).

To summarize, Bataille's fiction, at its most pornographic, is not reliant on the death or annihilation of women (the prostitute, however, is accorded such a dubious honour, as she is, as a subject, dead [*The Accursed Share*, vol. II, 143; *OC* VIII, 124]). Women, however, or 'Woman', do have a privileged relation to death and the erotic, which at times veers on making Woman the means to his end, his ending, his death, little and otherwise. The cunt is certainly a particular non-place, the place of death – and this surely can only be from the point of view of a subject who is not the woman in question (necessarily male only if we accept heterosexual psychoanalysis) and what in Bataille's fiction is it, such that the passage to the erotic or birth is the woman's to me than rather than to the woman herself. Beauty's role is to increase the woman's allure and although this could be read as a way of describing how modern Western culture sets store by feminine beauty, it is crucial that it is additionally a case, for his examples, simply about the idea of beauty. Beauty, the woman then comes to represent a question, something to be thought in terms of the [...]

'Woman' with regard to death, in Bataille's writing, and when seen in the light of what Bataille terms sovereignty (the loss of mastery), it may be that even the problematic aspects of women seeming to be part of 'his death' make women the more likely to accede to conditions like sovereignty. In one of Bataille's early texts, 'Solar Anus', we see the premonition of the paradox that occurs within sovereignty, the passage from mastery (sovereignty as usually understood). We read that

> I want to have my throat slashed while violating the girl to whom I will have been able to say: you are the night. [. . .] The *solar annulus* is the intact anus of her body at eighteen years to which nothing sufficiently blinding can be compared except the sun, even though the *anus* is the *night*. ('Solar Anus', 9; *OC* I, 86)

Death, rape, anal sex as the final possibility of mutual destruction – what could be seen as more 'problematic'? It is absolutely legitimate to question Bataille's imagery, his focus on the female body as a site of male subjectivity (the 'I' who wants this experience loses his self through the annulling of another's subjectivity), but we should always be asking how this fits into the general economy, the position of death within (or as) this economy, the place and function of eroticism, and how the individual loses its individuality in extreme behaviour. In this case there is no victor, only the loss of control, of individual sanctity for both; there is an equivalence in the undoing of the positions of power held before the encounter. Whether we accept this as enough to allow Bataille a certain number of suspect statements with regard to women is another question, but they can be justified as part of a whole process of thinking, if not always in their own right.

Notes

1. Compare this with 'death is the possibility of the absolute impossibility of *Dasein*' (Heidegger, *Being and Time*, 294), and 'that about which one has this anxiety [i.e. death] is simply *Dasein*'s potentiality-for-Being' (295). For Heidegger, death is definitive in its unattainability, thus making it inherent, and essential. Arguably Bataille strays into this terrain, but not willingly.

2. For Bataille's rendering of the relationship between death and architecture, see 'Architecture', 'Slaughterhouse' 'Museum'. Also 'The Obelisk'. For further

consideration of the role of models of building in (Hegel's) construction of Being, see Derrida, 'The Pit and the Pyramid: Introduction to Hegel's Semiology'.

3. On lines of demarcation between human and other, it is also worth noting the line between human and animal, broken in eroticism and at moments where conscious control of the organism fails or is broken down. Taboos often take the human/animal line as a key site of prohibition (see *The Accursed Share*, vol. II, 52, 90; *OC* VIII, 43, 78). In *Theory of Religion*, animality is described as an immanence that humanity escapes from, through transcendence (17–25; *OC* VII, 291–6). On the issue of death as origin, or in fact of there being in any real sense an origin to humanity, Bataille responds by writing that 'the only way we have to envisage the event is to do so as if things had taken place within the limits of a very short, virtually indivisible time span' (*The Accursed Share*, vol. II, 73; *OC* VIII, 62). So, on the one hand, I think it is possible to see that death is definitively 'the start of it all', and on the other that it is unknowable in its originality – this phenomenon being of the type that is called 'originary', in acknowledgement of this impossibility/difficulty.

On the question of taboo as such, for Bataille, taboo is inevitable, but there is no set form (*The Accursed Share*, vol. II, 29; *OC* VIII, 25). He specifically attacks Freud's *Totem and Taboo* in '17 janvier 1938' (*OC*, II, 281–7), saying that only one of its chapters is any good, and even that one gets the 'primitive' relation to death wrong (286). The precise reason for the incompatibility of Freud and Bataille can be see in statements such as the following: 'psychoanalysis has revealed that the totem animal is in reality a substitute for the father' (*Totem and Taboo*, 141). Freud is utterly unwilling to countenance a way of thinking that differs from the model based on universalizing the two-parent family. Bataille's exoticism is perhaps too open to what he believes to be other ways of thinking – he still uses the 'primitives' as a source of knowledge for 'us', but he is surely less 'orientalist' than Freud.

4. Paradoxically, whilst questioning the primacy of death in Blanchot, Gillian Rose brings us back to something like a notion of utility in death, death as foundation of utility (*Mourning Becomes the Law*, 101–23).

5. Such a conception, where death, sex, birth and anguish merge, is arguably

'Misérable' contains the sense of misery, in terms of sadness, and in terms of grinding poverty, and also the sense of something foul, nasty.

8. This concept features in Mona Hatoum's work, entitled *Corps étranger*, (1994) in which a video shows us the endoscopic camera she inserts in order to make a passage through her body. This piece is just one of many examples of the use made of abjection as a means of producing or thinking about art. Whether abjection can be *used* consciously is another question.

9. See 'Attraction and Repulsion II' and 'Attraction and Repulsion I: Tropisms, Sexuality, Laughter and Tears'.

10. Hal Foster develops an argument based on this difference, to account for how 'abject art' tries to be critical of abject society, or how it tries to respond to a condition of pre-existing abjection (Foster, *The Return of the Real*, 127–68, and 156 in particular).

11. For obvious examples where this is the case, see Hegel, *Phenomenology of Spirit*, Sartre, *Being and Nothingness* and Heidegger, *Being and Time*. For the critique of philosophy 'in the masculine' as being based on death and Freudian death drives, see Luce Irigaray, *Speculum of the Other Woman*, Hélène Cixous, 'Sorties', in *The Newly Born Woman*, 63–132, and Kristeva, *Powers of Horror* and *Tales of Love*.

12. For a careful analysis of gender and sexual positionings within and outside of, abjection, see Judith Still, 'Horror in Kristeva and Bataille: Sex and Violence'. This essay also stands as a powerful and concise rendering of the relationship contemporary feminisms (can) have with Bataille. See also Still, *Feminine Economies*.

13. Luce Irigaray, *The Irigaray Reader*, ed. Margaret Whitford. See also Elisabeth Bronfen, *Over Her Dead Body: Death, Femininity and the Aesthetic*, for a consideration of the largely male production of images of dead women.

14. See Andrea Dworkin, *Pornography: Men Possessing Women*, 167–74, for a summary of, essentially, the 'dirty bits' of *Story of the Eye*. For the critique of this 'reading', see Susan Rubin Suleiman, 'Pornography, Transgression and the Avant-Garde: Bataille's *Story of the Eye*'. Both Suleiman and Still (in 'Horror in Kristeva and Bataille') insist nonetheless on the need to consider the overt (explicit) content in Bataille's fiction, as well as the philosophical/theoretical/literary components.

15. See Still, 'Horror in Kristeva and Bataille', 229–30, for how such a process can appear in Bataille's *Madame Edwarda*.

16. In terms of references, I follow Still in 'Horror in Kristeva and Bataille', with regard to *My Mother/Madame Edwarda/The Dead Man*, in giving the page reference for the English version, while generally supplying my own translation. The translations of these three stories are so amusingly 'porno' compared to Bataille's texts that we can safely say Bataille would probably have enjoyed their abject risibility.

4

Sovereignty

Bataille's notion of sovereignty is what completes his theorization of a general economy. Although never published in his lifetime, *The Accursed Share,* vol. *III: Sovereignty* seems always to have been destined to be the conclusion. Of course, the general economy is not supposed to be a project, and cannot, in Bataille's logic, have a conclusion, as that would make it a system of utility, of means and ends – so sovereignty is the end which is not one. Sovereignty represents the status of the subject when caught up in general economy, and thus joins waste, expenditure, death, eroticism and so on as possible ends within such an economy. Even though to talk of ends still implies a project, and therefore

individual – but what happens is that you become enslaved to that moral, and the subject becomes a mere function of it (leaving aside the fact of social control in most morals). Bataille's notion of sovereignty tries to get outside these models, these *projects of utility*, by taking them to extremes, such that the subject can become all. But the subject can only be all in the instant, in the loss of self, or in death.

Sovereignty describes how the general economy infiltrates the subject individual of restricted economy (the world of knowable limits, knowledge, control, progress and projects), so that the subject falls away. Like all other aspects of the general economy, it operates retroactively such that it will also have always been at the supposed origin of the subject (the subject is based on the possibility of her/his non-existence or non-being). This is what undoes the sense of project that will emerge when looking at 'how sovereignty works' – for there are many occasions when it seems that sovereignty is something that can be acquired, at the end of a process of realization. The referral to sovereignty as always already there means more than saying 'in the beginning was the sovereign subject' – it is to say that, looking back, we deem it *now* to have always been there. On the other hand, in taking away the possibility of a sovereign subject as realization or achievement, sovereignty becomes the outside of the subject that infiltrates and always undoes the self-present subject that says 'I'.

Sovereignty is a form of process, nonetheless, and parallels the process begun in Hegel's *Phenomenology*. Where Hegel has a process which is all about ends, where Spirit – complete knowledge – is the end of everything, as absolute Being, Bataille has a process that mimics this, only to fall away, becoming nothing instead of something. This nothing is also not the something that defines 'when there is no thing present', but is the nothing that underpins how nothing relates to something, presence to absence, self to other. This process of sovereignty can be seen to begin with the death of God.

It is Nietzsche who is renowned as the writer of the 'death of God', and throughout *The Accursed Share*, vol. III, Nietzsche is presented as *the* writer of sovereignty – he expresses it directly, and stands for the *figure* of sovereignty, as, according to Bataille,

'Nietzsche's gift is the gift that nothing limits; it is the sovereign gift, that of subjectivity' (*The Accursed Share*, vol. III, 370; *OC* VIII, 404). In other words, Nietzsche's writing is the site where Nietzsche's own subjectivity is knowingly put at stake. If Nietzsche is exemplary in terms of approaching sovereignty, then a certain moment within his writing is exemplary in thinking 'what' sovereignty might be.

Whilst acknowledging that the third volume of *The Accursed Share* was not deemed complete enough to be published, and therefore far from definitive, it is interesting, and in my view highly important to look at an element which barely features in the final draft of the main text – the direct consideration of the death of God.[1] When Zarathustra announces the death of God (*Thus Spoke Zarathustra*, §3), man is left to his own devices, and becomes capable of genuine subjectivity. However, at exactly the same moment, subjectivity becomes impossible, because the guarantor of truth (and thus of identity) is gone. Nietzsche's declaration is historical – it 'represents' the secularization of thought, and society in general – but Zarathustra is speaking of something that is already the case but had not yet been noticed. Nietzsche also famously declares that 'nothing is true! Everything is permitted' (*On the Genealogy of Morals*, §III), and is often interpreted as meaning that the death of God entails the end of morals. Heidegger points out that 'nihilism is the history of the being itself, through which the death of the Christian God comes to light' (*Nietzsche*, vol. IV, 4). So Nietzsche's declarations can be

death of God does not become the certainty of atheism; it is the maintenance of the God as dead (*OC* VIII, 670n.), the living through the absence of God (677n.). Such a conception leads Bataille to the following statement:

> The sovereign feeling of death, of the absence of God, is the feeling of the unlimited absence of guarantees, and the hatred of all guarantees, which is the fate of sovereign existence. A sovereignty which serves no purpose is at the same time the coming apart and the completion of the human being. (651n.)

The possibility of a complete subjectivity is also, then, the removal of all bases and of all ultimate goals. Only those who are aware of the loss of God (and of all absolutes) can live sovereignly – the rest inhabit a servile existence even more wretched than before, as they are serving for serving's sake (in today's society, we might take the idea of efficiency being deemed an important goal as an example of this). Non-sovereign existence is part of the restricted economy – the domain that encompasses most of 'Western' society and insists on the necessity of subjugating everything to a position as means or end (which makes everything – and everybody – into a means). Non-sovereign existence includes those with power, who are caught within a master/slave relation of obligation, and servitude to their own power.

Sovereign existence is what Bataille's notion of general economy has been describing when it deals with a society based on sacrifice, or when considering the realm of eroticism and death. If sovereign is not a term that represents might, control, leadership ('the question of sovereignty is poorly formulated if we confuse it with the autonomous decision of an individual' (*The Accursed Share*, vol. III, 311; *OC* VIII, 349), it is in some ways a pinnacle to be attained (and lost at the same time). This is precisely in harmony with other movements in and of the general economy, where the new emphasis on waste does not preclude the existence of accumulation. As a working definition, we might say that *sovereignty is the general economy as it pertains to the individual (or subject)*, and if the paradigm for society is waste, then for the individual it is failure.

Sovereignty and Sovereign Existence

Sovereignty is to be regarded as a process – one that is about completion, and the necessary failure to attain completion. This does not stop Bataille from making a host of statements along the lines of 'sovereignty is . . .'. In looking at the constellation of such assertions, we can, I believe, find a dispersal of certainty, exactly as we can in the writings of Nietzsche, and this fragmentation that comes with 'the whole' is part of what sovereignty is about.

Sovereignty emerges as the dissolving of the subject and object worlds, and in some way represents the overcoming of the divide (*The Accursed Share*, vol. II, 112–13; *OC* VIII, 97–8). This has led some writers, such as Jean-Luc Nancy in *The Inoperative Community*, to argue that Bataille still has a notion that there is such a thing as an autonomous subject, even if this is not the be-all and end-all. Such a view neglects the line Bataille develops, which is that what we *do* have is the *belief* that we are autonomous subjects (and are therefore objects to and of thought), and unlike Hegel, Bataille emphasizes the contingency of such a state, as sovereignty can come and undo any autonomy, any identity (he also emphasizes the contingency of sovereignty itself). Sovereignty is also beyond the profane world (the world of autonomous individuals) in that it aspires to the sacred – the sacred as 'horror, anguish, death' (*The Accursed Share*, vol. II, 169; *OC* VIII, 146), rather than the sacred in the form of an object (the 'sole Subject' as object – God).

seem, at moments, to have existed before, as, he states, 'sovereignty is man's primordial condition, his basic condition' (284; 325), even if 'lost' (197; 247). Also, sovereignty would provide a 'deep subjectivity' (234; 280).

Thus far it seems that Bataille is proposing a more authentic form of subjectivity, one that is less alienated than our current *restricted* existence, and that we have had this before, and could do so again. He suggests that sovereigns in the traditional sense were in some way nearer to sovereignty than we are today, and that societies based on sacrifice also had a privileged relation to sovereignty.[3] Bataille's continued restating of the impossibility of restoring a lost sovereignty is important in assessing this: 'we can only go further, without imagining for a moment the possibility of a going back' (228; 275). I take this to include the impossibility of either a return to human sacrifice or of there being a real subject to be restored once the mundane world has been thrown off.

The 'deep subjectivity' cited above is basically an empty one (and if it looks significant to us, it is mentioned only fleetingly by Bataille) – it is nothing to do with knowledge, even knowledge of death. It is not the overcoming of death, but the living in death that threatens knowledge and the subject. Sovereignty 'is essentially the refusal to accept the limits that the fear of death would have us respect' (221, 269), and 'the sovereign is he who *is* as if death were not' (222; 270). At this stage, it appears that the sovereign individual might be one who breaks all laws, and has no fear of death – and to an extent, this is an element (Sade features as someone who approached sovereignty). However, it is the everyday world that is filled with death as

> the sovereign world does have an odour of death, but this is for the subordinate man; for the sovereign man, it is the world of practice that smells bad; if it does not smell of death, it smells of anguish; its crowds sweat from the anguish provoked by shadows; death exists in a contained state, but fills it up. (222; 270)

The sovereign moment, however, is one which, in losing the limits of subjectivity, loses the limit – death – as well. Death, has, in some way, to be gone through: the experience of 'death reduc[ing] to NOTHING the individual who took himself, and whom others took for a thing identical to itself' (216; 264) must be undergone. In going through death as limit, we do not learn anything or improve ourselves – we would merely, for an instant, be in sovereignty – except that you cannot *be* in sovereignty.

Bataille defines sovereignty again, 'as *the miraculous reign of unknowing*' (444n.; 252n.), as sovereignty is impossibility, and an impossibility that infects the 'realm of knowing'. Sovereignty is about the loss of all knowledge, and of all possibility, in the sense of ends and means, and this loss occurs at the *height* of knowledge – climbing Hegel's edifice, Bataille seeks to fall, and only the fall is sovereign: not the preliminaries, not the will to fall, not watching the fall, not watching the result of the fall. Only the moment of loss: 'unlimited knowledge is *the knowledge* [*savoir*] of NOTHING' (439n.; 251n.). Later he restates that 'the passage from knowledge to unknowing is not a moment of composition; it is a decomposition of thought' (453n.; 403n.). The moment of unknowing is a moment only, and is not a gain, in the way religious mystics, for example, might understand such a thing, and in order to clarify this, we need to pause on the term 'NOTHING' that Bataille uses.

NOTHING is written in capitals in order to distinguish it from terms such as 'the void' or nothingness. Such terms allow critics of what they call 'nihilism' to assert that nihilists do believe in something – even if this something is only the truth of nothingness. NOTHING is Bataille's recognition of the difficulty in looking at what is other than our limited existence (recalling that 'limited' is not a value judgement, as value judgements belong to the limited/restricted economy). Its excessive character shows it trying to get beyond 'the void' whilst also failing even to be the void.

always surrounds our being anyway), but it seems that this moment of decomposition must occur. For Bataille, it is not enough to say the subject does not really exist; the non-existence of the subject must be brought about. He writes that at the sovereign moment, 'I would no longer know, [when] my initial anticipation would dissolve into NOTHING' (208; 258).

This collapsing into 'NOTHING' is significantly different from a cut-rate nihilism which asserts that nothing is true, and therefore nothing *is* true. Nietzsche does not think this, and neither does Bataille. The former writes of the levels of illusion, of the 'apparent' world, and argues that the loss of a true world means we might just have the world of appearances. For Nietzsche, there is appeal to a truth (even empty) behind the appearances but there is nothing *behind* either 'truth' or 'appearance' (*Twilight of the Idols*, 25). This lack of both something (there are only appearances) and nothing (there are only appearances, not a void behind them) is what Bataille is aspiring to in his use of the term NOTHING, as this is designed to exclude the 'true' nothingness of the universe as much as the 'true' truth of the universe. In excluding them, he also brings them back in. In other words, as with Nietzsche, nothing is true, but *that is why anything or everything exists*.

So, NOTHING is both more and less than 'nothingness' or 'the void' (le néant). However, at this point, we might still be tempted to believe that NOTHING constitutes some sort of answer to 'what the universe is'. Bataille specifies that NOTHING is the kind of answer that is not one, that is the lack of the answer, and the *necessary* failure (not rejection) of the goal of 'being the universe', or of being a subject. NOTHING is the impossibility of impossibility, i.e. the impossibility of *being* where being *is not*, but also the impossibility of our existence. If death is 'the negative miraculous' (207; 257), then so is life.

This intertwining brings us back to the general economy of waste and excess: the NOTHING Bataille valorizes occupies the same position in his theory as the sacrifices of the Aztecs – it does seem to be a better thing than our miserable everyday existence, but it infiltrates this existence anyway. It may not always be in form of the total loss of self, but could certainly be in the loss of knowledge, or refusal of linear logic.

In fact, in case the impression is given that Bataille is pursuing a purely individualistic vision in the third volume of *The Accursed Share*, it should be noted that huge sections of the book are devoted to the Stalinist Soviet Union. Politically, Bataille finds Marxism too dogmatic, so his awareness of the brutalities of the Soviet Union should prevent him from being an apologist for Stalinism, and yet that is precisely what he becomes. As if aware that he really has not addressed the *general* aspect of sovereignty, he opts to describe the society which at least can claim something utopian, even if only as the 'best of a bad lot'. Stalinism is part of sovereignty because it renounces the bourgeois fallacy of the subject individual, wherein the individual is not sovereign but part of a 'society of things' (*The Accursed Share*, vol. III, 345; *OC* VIII, 381). Stalinism continues this, but without the pretence of the individual, of freedom through that individual's 'choice': 'it is the bourgeois debasement of sovereign subjectivity that communism destroys' (360; 395). This is all well and good, and the perspective that a reduction in freedom is nearer to sovereignty is interesting, *but* communism under Stalin is totally about the future – individuals do not give themselves up in some potlatch of community, but in the service of the future 'communist' State. It strikes me that sovereignty is presumably supposed to be as much about losing object status as in losing subjectivity, and literally life, and would fit strangely with what Stalinism was actually, rather than notionally up to.

Bataille recommends that at the social level we pursue communism, and at an individual level follow Nietzsche into a dispersal of subjectivity whilst attempting to be Godlike – and Bataille has in

The more purely philosophical Bataille gets, the nearer he approaches the complexities of Blanchot's variant on phenomenology, and awareness of this, alongside a reading of Bataille that lets his text assert truths which cannot actually be true for him, is, for me, the way to approach the difficult (or apparently simple) and seemingly contradictory parts of his writing. On issues such as 'the impossibility of being' for example, it is advisable to stay away from words like contradiction, and instead to think about paradoxes (except where he tries to link Stalinism with what else he has to say about the general economy).[5] The paradoxical element in Bataille is possibly at its most evident in *Inner Experience*, written at about the same time as *The Accursed Share*, if 'finished' earlier. *Inner Experience*, part of Bataille's 'other trilogy' – the *Somma Atheologica* (also including *Guilty* and *On Nietzsche*), is in fact very close to what occurs in the theorization of the general economy, particularly in the thought of sovereignty, and is perhaps the height of Bataille's phenomenology, insofar as that is what he might be up to. Its focus on the individual is what links it to Kierkegaard and Sartre (who vigorously attacked it). I wish to present it as a parallel to *The Accursed Share*, vol. III, which I think helps put some distance between it and the sub-phenomenology of existentialism.

Inner Experience and the Loss of Self

Experience is a peculiar term to find lurking in a writer seen to be a major precursor of philosophies that reject traditional notions of subjectivity, and, like many of Bataille's usages, it is not quite what we usually understand by the word 'experience' that is at stake here. In fact, it is the usual meaning of the term that is *at stake*, under threat. For Bataille, 'inner experience' is neither inner, nor is it subjective experience: instead it is the experience of what is other (Nancy, *The Inoperative Community*, 18). It refers solely to the experiencing of the limits of the subject – in other words, where experience, particularly as continuity or narrative, breaks down, or attains its limit. The term experience persists as 'one must *live* experience' (*Inner Experience*, 8; *OC* V, 21), so it is a deviation, rather than a simple rejection of the usual meaning of experience. The experience (and *expérience* also includes the notion of experimentation) is not the living, but what is to be lived, and this experience consists of anguish and ecstasy – all that drives the self-present subject, that knows its identity, away (4, 12; 16, 24). It is therefore a process, a process of loss (xxxii-iii; 10–11) rather than an accumulation, just as with the general economy.

This experience is 'inner' because it is to be further distinguished from experience as 'what happens in the world, and how we process it', thus making it a radical phenomenology that exceeds Heidegger's notion of *Dasein* (the being of Being). It is 'inner' because it comes from within the boundaries of the individual, but only to break those boundaries: hence the emphasis on 'ecstasy' – being outside oneself. This 'being outside oneself' becomes, in the long run, the reason why *Inner Experience* is the account of a failure, the impossibility of attaining excess by oneself.

'Inner experience' is a project to undo projects (22; 35). The individual, seeking to make his or her self the measure of the universe – to become the Subject – can only attain this through losing the self, and in losing the self, the becoming absolute is destined to fail – since there will be no self left if you become equal to 'everything'. In practical terms, insofar as such an idea applies, Bataille's method consists of confronting the nothingness outside (death, the absence of God, the absence of self), and embracing this (see 72; 87, where he writes that the relation to death is like an erotic relation, not one of knowledge), rather than knowing it – this is what leads to the stress put on anguish: it is too much for the indi-

end will have become worthless) from the 'summit' of thought – in other words, the project for full subjectivity must be in play, for it to be disassembled *as it attains itself*: the height of subjectivity, for Bataille, is the absence of such a thing, and then the comical absence of the absence, so the 'negative miraculous' here is that there is something rather than nothing, and this something is rather less than nothing: it is NOTHING. The writer Bataille is closest to here is Beckett.[6] The latter is renowned for the staging of something very similar to the 'negative miraculous', and responses that do more and less than acknowledge futility.[7]

To sum up, the experience of the subject proposed by Bataille is one where the subject falls away, into nothingness, risibility and silence. God is noted in his absence, and also refused as being part of the bid to make the sacred into something useful, a thing (*Guilty*, 16; *OC* V, 250– 1). There is to be no answer at the end of the process: 'you must not believe that truth lies in the void' (*OC* V, 577n.). What have occurred 'along the way' (but not in a way that can be incorporated into a narrative) are the moments of sovereign existence, where inner experience is 'the being without delay' (*Inner Experience*, 47; *OC* V, 60) – so there has not been any accumulation of Being (in the form of standard experience), as being *is* delay, deferral – as evidenced in the saying/writing of 'I' – there is always a gap between the 'being' and the saying of being. Bataille offers an immanent Being which is not one that can actually be lived by the subject: it occurs in moments of erotic abandon, drunkenness, laughter. In general, it occurs when the subject is lost in community or communication (12, 24; 24, 37). For this reason, *Inner Experience* fails (and sovereignty is about failure, not success) on more than one count: it fails because, if we believe Bataille, it must, but also because it reveals the fallacy that heightened (non)subjectivity can be approached in isolation (as existentialism would have it). Only a limited subjectivity exists in isolated individuals – individuals who are not in any sense really isolated, but are isolated through the demands of reality, i.e. the belief that our freedom and reality lies in our separatedness).[8]

The failure that is *Inner Experience* has a further, 'communicative' element, and that is the one contained in the writing of the text. Bataille does suggest the existence of a superior reality that writing cannot match, and that the writing of 'inner experience' is only going to seem ridiculous (see, for example, 60; 75). Nonetheless, the writing is part of the undoing of any authenticity for the experience, as it adds another layer of distance from the hope of truth – and the experience only exists in the form of not being the writing, or the conscious *thought* of experience. At a more banal level, the text is in some ways designed as a set of suggestions for and observations on methods for attaining (and then losing) subjectivity, and is more effective when taken in this light, because the reading of experience is all we can have – we can never know it, even if we 'attain' it. When viewed from more of a distance, *Inner Experience* fails in uninteresting, as well as in theoretically interesting ways, in that it seems to want to be manual, and is too beholden to existence as project, in ways that later texts are not.

Écriture and Sovereignty

Derrida's interest in Bataille has proved essential in the processing of Bataille's writing. In 'From Restricted to General Economy' Derrida undertakes a detailed reading of Bataille through the latter's engagement and disengagement with Hegel. Derrida focuses on the notion of sovereignty, and distances it from mastery, while specifying that sovereignty is not simply the opposite of mastery, or the outside of dialectics ('From Restricted to General Economy', 260–1). It is the outside of dialectics only insofar as

writes that 'it is at a general level, as an authentic movement, preg-
nant with meaning, that we must talk of the "failure" of Hegel'
(334n., trans. mod.).[9] Derrida emphasizes that Hegel has not really
failed, for Bataille, but this goes against the position of 'failure' in
Bataille's writing on sovereignty: 'failure' does not mean a simple
lack of success, but the failure that *does* occur at the height of
thought (the system, the truth, the Subject), as the only possible
'success'.

In a later note, Derrida fails to pursue Bataille's very strong
implication that Hegel did more than in some way realize that his
system had to have an outside, and in fact quite simply turned his
back on the difficulties Bataille is determined to live through and
in. Bataille writes:

> Hegel, I imagine, touched the extreme. He was still young and thought
> he would go mad. I even imagine that he elaborated the system in
> order to escape (any kind of conquest, doubtless, is due to a man flee-
> ing a danger). To conclude, Hegel reaches *satisfaction* and turns his
> back on the extreme. (*Inner Experience*, 43; *OC* V, 56; cited by Derrida,
> 'From Restricted to General Economy', 334n.)

Derrida even continues the quotation further, but seems oblivious
to the contempt shown by Bataille for Hegel's systematizing the
'restricted economy', even while he acknowledges the requirement
to 'go through' what Hegel does produce. This could be considered
the 'blind spot' of Derrida's own text, a blind spot that serves to
structure his impending argument that Bataille's notion of sovereignty is 'all about writing'.[10]

Derrida is exceptionally positive in his reading of Bataille in this
essay, and this is perhaps because it provides the material for one
of his own major ideas, that of *écriture*, or writing. He argues that
Bataille's notion of sovereignty is one that comes to pass in writing,
as writing marks the death of the writer, community with the other,
and the risk of loss of meaning. What is also important is the notion
of 'slippage' of terms, or of their 'sliding' from one meaning to
another ('From Restricted to General Economy', 262–3). Notions
can also slip from one word to another, so, for example, in the
'method of meditation' which follows *Inner Experience*, meditation
comes to replace 'inner experience', thus undermining the suspi-
cion that there was a truth as the possible end product of *Inner*

Experience. So Bataille does not let us settle, opting instead for a 'potlatch of signs' ('From Restricted to General Economy', 262). Transgression, the breaking out of restricted existence, has its 'place' in this disruptive language, more subtle than Joyce, and seemingly too excessive for Beckett, there is yet something of both in Bataille's expression of subjectivity in, across and out of language.

Derrida's essay is an exemplary reading of Bataille, all the more impressive for effectively predicting bits of Bataille's texts (the *Œuvres complètes* were not as yet published), but (as noted in Chapter 2 above) we should be wary of Derrida's hurry to reduce Bataille to 'writing', no matter how broad a concept we have of such a term, as Bataille's writing is the writing that undoes writing in the everyday sense (even for Derrida) in its stress on immanence, and its own meaninglessness. In later texts, Derrida makes passing reference to Bataille, and these too have proved influential. The most striking example is Bataille's positioning as just one more philosopher with the sun at the centre of his system of metaphors.[11] This despite Bataille, from the beginning, with 'Solar Anus', clearly problematizing the centrality of sun and light *at the same time as he keeps it in the centre*.[12] To summarize, Derrida's engagement with Bataille has been both positive and negative for the latter, with there being a danger of Bataille's thought being subsumed into Derrida's. For either writer, loss of identity and property is vital in their philosophy, but we should not mistake or lessen the significance of the appearance (and then disappearance) of the proper name 'Bataille' in the

2. Sovereignty as a historical concept has also undergone its own 'death of God', such that even if some monarchs are seen by Bataille to have been to some degree sovereign, they no longer can be, once 'being the sovereign' comes to be about holding power, rather than about being the embodiment of the people, especially in sacrifice. This longstanding and seemingly counter-intuitive relation of sovereignty to actual sovereigns (in that they were limited by the power they held) means that eventually all can 'be' sovereign, as monarchs never truly were sovereign, and developments from the French Revolution on have removed even the illusion of sovereignty. The death of God is democratic in its way, but it is the democracy of death that is closest to sovereignty.

3. Bataille tackles this question throughout *The Accursed Share*, and in the third volume in particular. (See *The Accursed Share*, vol III, 237–57; *OC* VIII, 283–301.) No definitive answer emerges, and perhaps cannot, as Bataille's examples are exemplary rather than making truth claims.

4. See also *On Nietzsche*, where Bataille specifically praises *Ecce Homo* for 'affirm[ing] the absence of a goal, the insubordination of the author to any plan' (*OC* VI, 22).

5. Nancy argues that this problem, which Bataille thinks is a paradox, is one that arises out of a mistake about individual subjects and their relation to community. Nancy argues that rather than there being subjects (however contingent they really are) who then lose themselves in (a) community, community is the process in all individuals, and individuals are the process of community (*The Inoperative Community*, 23–5). I introduce this view here because Nancy has chosen to ignore the *College of Sociology* writings in favour of the writings on sovereignty, as a base for his critique. In essence, Nancy's view is parallel to that of Habermas, where all of our communications are defined in a community, and understanding is part of this. So, for Nancy, not only is Bataille mistaken to introduce Stalinism into the equation, he is actually wrong to think about sovereignty in the way that he does.

6. See Critchley, *Very Little, Almost Nothing*, for a comprehensive rendering of the parallels between Bataille, Blanchot and Beckett. Bataille wrote little on Beckett, but there are many moments when he writes on 'silence', trying to write silence itself, in the process. See the closing chapter below.

7. Bataille returns, over and over, to silence: 'the sovereign silence' ('Méthode de méditation', *OC* V, 210. See also *Inner Experience*, 29, 76; *OC* V, 42, 91 for examples). Silence is what lies beyond discourse, and is always less than an answer, and part of a process. Silence is the failure to speak, but also the failure to *be* and to be *silent*.

8. An individual can approach community through the 'experience' of the void, even if this cannot be retained, so it does not have to be with other people that the communication occurs – it can be with all that is 'other'. Bataille also offers the term 'le pal' as a variant on this 'communing' with (or in) the nothingness of being. This 'being impaled' is the painful, degrading awareness that is the loss of awareness and subjectivity. (See *On Nietzsche*, 63–4; *OC* VI, 78–9.)

9. The original translation has totally altered the emphasis of the sentence, undoing the force that remains in 'failure', even with its inverted commas. The

original reads as follows: 'C'est généralement, comme d'un mouvement authentique et lourd de sens, qu'il faut parler de l' "échec" de Hegel' (Bataille, 'Hegel, la mort et le sacrifice' ('Hegel, Death and Sacrifice') *OC*, XII, 344; cited by Derrida, 'De l'économie restreinte à l'économie générale', *L'Écriture et la différence*, 372).

10. Paul de Man has commented that this is how Derrida's writing works – he creates a distance between the 'object' writer and text, only to bring them together. De Man argues that Derrida identified what he did in Rousseau because Rousseau had actually made the argument already (see 'The Rhetoric of Blindness: Jacques Derrida's Reading of Rousseau').

There is another sense in which sovereignty can be construed as being about, or at least occurring in, writing: this is through the work of those writers who aspire to take us beyond our closed subjectivity into a form of loss that they themselves have experienced. Hence the importance, above all, of Nietzsche, but also of all the writers dealt with in *Literature and Evil*. Rimbaud also features as someone whose renouncing of writing is of sovereign 'value' (see *OC* III, 533n.).

11. See Derrida, 'Economimesis' (particularly 11), and 'White Mythology', *Margins of Philosophy*, 271.

12. Incidentally, as well as Derrida's progressive forgetting of Bataille (he comes to write an entire book – *Given Time I: Counterfeit Money* – on 'the gift' and its problems without mentioning Bataille), there is often an attribution to Derrida of Bataille's theories. For example, Alan Bass, in his notes for 'White Mythology', summarizes what the general economy is 'for Derrida' (*Margins of Philosophy*, 209). He does not mention Bataille, despite clearly outlining the latter's theory. What is particularly instructive in this case is that Derrida's text makes no mention of 'general economy' as a term.

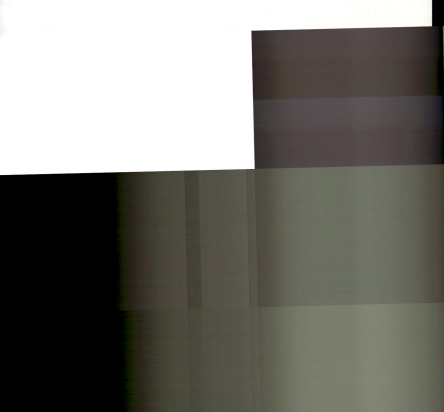

5

Community and Sacrifice

Bataille's conception of the individual, as it appears within 'sovereignty', the general economy, and/or in 'inner experience', is of an individual who undoes their subjectivity. This 'individual' could feasibly take one of two directions with regard to communities. In the first place, such an individual is even less likely to be part of a group than an individual *subject* who would be identified by their self-presence and agency. Alternatively, the dissolved individual might be a totally social creature, merging with the community as opposed to being the isolated individual beloved of liberalism.

Typically enough, Bataille takes the individual into both of these possibilities, in what looks like a dialectical synthesis: the sovereign individual is by definition not isolated. In *Eroticism*, it is clear that inner experience is most likely to occur with others, in some form or another (97–100; *OC* X, 98–101), and as Nancy noted, 'inner experience' is neither inner nor is it experience. This 'experience of the other' can also be sovereign, when it too refuses closure, rejects *knowing* the other. The endpoint of Bataille's idea of community is such a coming together – one that threatens what we normally term community (as an expression of togetherness, unity, self-awareness, shared practices), and the paradigm for this community is sacrifice, and all that surrounds it. But if community in sacrifice is the endpoint, the starting point for the thought of community in Bataille is far simpler in its conception, even if sacrifice and loss can, in hindsight, be seen to be issues at the start.

This chapter takes in Bataille's early statements of community, and follows them through to their conclusion in *Eroticism* and in the erotic fiction. In Bataille's writings we can trace a progress of the thought of community, from the 1930s, where it is most clearly apparent in the literal practice of sacrifice, through *Somma Atheologica/Inner Experience*, where loss of the self and going beyond the self cause 'communication'. Finally, we can see the thought become perhaps more obviously communal in *Eroticism*, where loss of the self is part of what Bataille terms 'continuity' (this notion develops from 'intimacy' in *The Accursed Share*).

The simplest version of community in Bataille is that of a group of people operating as a society. In addition, he develops a clear conception of an 'elective community', which operates at several levels (for example in terms of the 'sense of community' one might have with certain writers, or, equally, the development of an 'actually existing' communal group). From here, it is a question of what kind of community he is suggesting, and I think it will become apparent that this is more than a question of 'who will be let in', as it comes to encompass exactly *how* we form a community. In fact, the how is the what, where, who and why of Bataille's community. The next stage sees a community as that which surpasses the individual, but also surpasses society, as the occurrence of genuine community is at the *moment* where the mundane, or even profane, society is undone (on the occasion of sacrifice, for example).

integrationist liberalism, which seeks to homogenize while 'accepting' people from 'outside of its culture'.

Beyond the Individual

As with his writings specifically on the general economy, Bataille is consistently attacking the modern conception of the individual as being the or even a centre of knowledge and truth. In his attacks on the uses made of people through the restricted economies of truth assertions (e.g. religions, philosophies that believe in essential truths) or of the capitalist economy, he is not advocating the dis-alienation of an otherwise complete human. However, something like an individual can, it seems, be better off in what we might think of as a dis-alienated community (hence his continued interest in the possibilities of communism). From early texts such as the two 'Attraction and Repulsion' essays, the essays on 'The Pineal Eye', through the *Accursed Share*, and still present in the late texts *Eroticism* and *The Tears of Eros*, Bataille is at pains to get the individual beyond 'its' self. In the process, he is led to consider societies that gave more scope to such possibilities than 'ours' does. The societies that come out well invariably feature an element of sacrifice, and certainly require a sacred that we no longer have – this sacred is not to be confused with the workings of religion, whose task it is to control the sacred; Bataille is interested in the moments when the sacred irrupts into being and is beyond the bounds of our attempts to organize it.

An example that he returns to over and over again is that of the Aztecs – the first real consideration being as early as 1928 ('L'Amérique disparue', ['Vanished America'] *OC* I, 152–8). The importance of their civilization is that they had a genuine place for the sacred, a sacred that goes beyond observance of certain rules, because the moment of the sacred is brought into being *as those rules are broken* – i.e. in (human) sacrifice. Christianity is also based on such sacrifice, but in sanitizing the procedure (through rendering the sacrifice 'symbolic'), the sacred aspect has been lost; hence the contribution of Christianity to a 'profanation' of the world, the results of which can be seen in capitalism and individualism. Societies that are able to suspend their laws do so in the festival (fête), and Bataille argues that this is the moment when the society becomes a community.

Many writers, and we can take Hegel and Heidegger as paradigmatic in this context, would have argued that society/community occurs through a process of negativity, and that an awareness of death is what sets humanity apart *as* humanity (even if we hardly needed to wait for phenomenology to find this out) and drives us to react against this initial negativity, by creating society as protection. The next stage in the argument is that society is quite literally *built* on death (hence Neanderthal man coming gradually to be seen as human, due to the discovery of marked burial sites).[1] Bataille would accept this, I would argue, but sees it as a defence mechanism that allows itself to fail at certain points (in the festival, eroticism, laughter, drunkenness, sacrifice), and that community does not grow up huddled together fending off death, but happens in and through death. Once death is to be kept outside at all times, then the sacred has vanished, and this has gradually come about, notably through Christianity.

He allows, for example, that the Christian village church does still have vestiges of the sacred, in that it encourages both fear (those who are buried there, not touching certain holy items) and longing for proximity (in the minimal 'communion') – attraction and repulsion.[2] Nonetheless, this is a weak form of the sacred, as it does not lead to its own dissolution. In other words its communal aspect, that of bringing together 'the faithful', is perhaps social, but is not, in Bataille's terms, community. Christianity is one of

For a society to be something that allowed community, in the Bataillean sense, to occur, it would have to be an 'elective community' – one that was together not by accident, but one that was linked organically *in its belief that community was what was beyond society's everyday existence*. This 'community' would not *be* a Bataillean community, but would allow the prospect of its intrusion. These elective communities can come from within a society, and are part of a process through which society develops:

> new communities combine with the old organization – the one stemming only from blood or the soil – and sometimes they will even become more important [. . .]. From then on [such a community] can be regarded as one of the communities forming society and take the name of *traditional* community, differing from the new communities, the most important of which are the *elective* communities. ('Sacred Sociology', 81; *OC* II, 301)

Clearly what Bataille is calling 'traditional' could be seen as elective *at some point* – for example, if we were following a story of society being based on a social contract – otherwise there has to be a claim that there would be a naturalized (if now to be deemed inferior) level of society based on 'blood or the soil'. Hollier's note here adds a useful precision as to what kind of community is elective (and he refers to the actual College of Sociology as being Bataille et al.'s attempt at such a community):

> The College refuses to belong to de facto communities. The elective communities that it opposes to them, communities of persons brought together by elective affinities, could be defined as communities of value. What value? Precisely that of the community as such: a community of those for whom the community is a value and not a fact. One's country is only a fact: it would be stupid to deny it, it is morally inadmissible to limit oneself to it. (Hollier, *The College of Sociology*, 407n.)

This comment highlights several key points: the existence or otherwise of a society-wide sacred is not a barrier to one coming into existence as a momentary thing. Members of communities could be both traditional and elective *at different times*. The problem is that 'elective' comes to sound far too voluntarist – how are we to get out of the traditional society (i.e. the society of norms, rules and traditions, whatever they might be), how are we able to make such a choice? Why should elective communities today choose in any way to adopt or mirror what traditional societies have done? Perhaps the link is that priesthoods and secret societies would in some way always have been elective communities – and it is worth bearing in mind that belonging to such a community is still not 'community' in the full Bataillean sense.

In more immediate terms, when addressing the College of Sociology, Bataille is thinking of the possibilities at the time – how the College, and its hidden double, *Acéphale*, might move towards a contemporary practice of the sacred. Much is also made of the community that forms around Bataille, Caillois, Leiris and many others, as being exemplary of a working method that itself hinted at going beyond the individual (as with dada in its various manifestations in particular cities a few years earlier). In addition, there are the very close intellectual links that go largely unstated, between Bataille and Blanchot during the war, Bataille and Colette Peignot in the late 1930s, and that Bataille also had with Benjamin, Lacan and Weil. But it is not enough to say that this indicates the significance of community – what matters is that many of these thinkers share a view of community that is other than the unity and cohesion generally implied in the term. This version of intellectual community extends to writers outside the present time – and to Nietzsche in particular (see *Inner Experience*, 26–7; *OC* V, 39, and also *OC* V, 436n.). It also extends to readers (of Bataille) who, in his absence, will ideally experience this community, which is absence of community (see *Inner Experience*, 60–1; *OC* V, 75, and Blanchot, *The Unavowable Community*, 23).[3]

shall argue more fully in the next section. If community is not about 'everyone coming together', then it is not about harmonious existence either – so while communism would wipe out the anti-excesses of capitalism, it is not enough of an answer, as it is sufficient, not excessive. So far, we have only looked at what essentially are standard ideas about community. It is when these receive further development that Bataille's notion becomes something different.

Community in the Loss of Community

Even though many alternative views of community co-exist, in some form, in Bataille, his statement of intent would be that he was in search of the 'negative community: the community of those that do not have one' (*OC* V, 483n.). If this is how he describes his 'projects' for community, it also applies to what community might be at the moment of its occurrence – and that is: nothing (or NOTHING, perhaps). Community is to be found at something like the centre, but strangely unattainable – it is the 'nucleus of violent silence' ('Attraction and Repulsion II', 114; *OC* II, 319) – so in the example of a Christian church it would be seen as the heart of a community, but for Bataille, the community is in the actual sacred (the experience of sacrifice, death, ecstatic ritual) – that which is held apart, but also worryingly nearby.[4]

This duality builds on Durkheim's conception (in *Elementary Forms*) of the sacred as being both pure and impure (and glossed by Caillois, in *L'Homme et le sacré*), to add a spatial dimension of 'attraction and repulsion', such that we try to separate off the sacred (removing the dead, keeping what is holy untouchable, putting gods above, and so on), but are so drawn to it that it returns to cause anguish. The spatial conception of the sacred is an attempt to account for our anguish and fear of certain things, whilst suggesting that this anguish is in fact a process including our avoidance – doomed to failure as it is. A diminished form of this persists in fiction, or for example, horror films, where even though we might be comforted by a resolution, that never erases the instants of shock, or fear (*The Accursed Share*, vol. II, 109; *OC* VIII, 94).[5] In 'real life', organizations such as religions provide the comfortable resolution, while the sacred remains a hidden threat, as with excess in the world of restricted economy.

In the writings of the 1930s, Bataille is keen to stress that community is at stake in moments of social crisis, as on the one hand, the forces of increased order try to take control, while on the other, the prospect for genuine community (more than just living together) emerges. Clearly this is occurring in the context of Fascism, and the search for possible alternatives. For Bataille, it was not enough to just 'fight Fascism' – whatever it was responding to was deeper than economic conditions, or simple political imperatives – Fascism was tapping into something like the sacred, in the same way as it took up Nietzsche. The following, exemplary, statement of this position (in capitals in the original) comes from one of the essays on Nietzsche from this period:

> The critical phase of a civilization's decomposition is regularly followed by a recomposition, which develops in two different directions: the reconstitution of religious elements of civil and military sovereignty, tying existence to the *past*, is followed or accompanied by the birth of free and liberating sacred figures and myths, *renewing* life. ('Nietzschean Chronicle', 206; *OC* I, 483)

The reference to myths is not to be understated either, as for Bataille all we have are myths, and myths are superior to truth, in that they are not statements of fact but are statements of community ('The Sorcerer's Apprentice', 232; *OC* I, 535). Bataille will also link an 'absence of myth' ('The Surrealist Religion', 81, *OC* VII, 393) *as myth* to an 'absence of community' (81; 393–4), when speaking of

taboo against murder, and the ecstatic encounter with the sacred would not be the same if we simply were 'at one with it'. The following statement shows how the intrusion of death provides a form of necessary energy:

> The death of an individual can be considered one of the most alarming expenditures for human beings united in a group. The corpse is treated, in fact, as a reality that could threaten to spread. Moreover, as the counterpart of the tendency to limit expending forces, there exists a tendency to expend, even to expend as much force as possible and eventually to the point of complete loss. *And it is impossible to imagine an energetic movement within a human group not comprising such a central expenditure of force.* ('Attraction and Repulsion II', 123; *OC* II, 331, my emphasis)

We therefore need crime to exist, for the laws to be broken, Law to be suspended. As in *The Accursed Share*, there does seem to be a great need to engage with death, horror, anguish and so on, such that it seems we can elect to approach the sacred more or less (as a society). Modern societies tend to not approach it at all, whilst 'primitive' societies approach it at moments of collective loss, which is how a real community is formed:

> Without free loss, without expense of energy, no collective existence, or even individual existence is possible. Consequently, as human beings we cannot live without breaking the barriers we must give to our need to expend, barriers that look no less frightening than death. (123; 331)

Sacrifice satisfies this supposed need, as it brings us together in order to make us lose ourselves in the process of law-breaking. The question remains as to whether a new body is created that would supersede us as individuals at such a time. Bataille's emphasis on loss suggests otherwise; he argues that transcendence is a limit on the sacred, not its realization:

> Christianity has made the sacred *substantial*, but the nature of the sacred, in which today we recognize the burning existence of religion, is perhaps the ungraspable thing that has been produced between men: the sacred is only a privileged moment of communal unity, a moment of the convulsive communication of what is ordinarily stifled.
>
> Such a disjunction between the sacred and transcendental substance (consequently impossible to create) suddenly opens a new field – a field perhaps of violence, perhaps of death. ('The Sacred', 242; *OC* I, 562–3)[6]

The moment that the sacred occurs is one of contagion, as opposed to a holistic unity – it spreads and takes us over, rather than us 'becoming one with it', and this contagion is the basis (or *is*) the communication Bataille is writing about. Once the moment passes, we have the standard version of community – as a reaction to the moment of loss, we try to master it (only for this mastering to exist under the threat of its dissolution).

Contagion can also occur in more straightforward situations than those involving actual sacrifice. Throughout his writings, Bataille valorizes laughter as a version of loss, of excess – where rational control slips (in notes for *The Accursed Share*, he writes that 'expenditure is contagious' [*OC* VII, 596n.]). In *Inner Experience*, we have the example of laughter as contagion. Bataille argues that in watching something that makes us laugh (whether designed to or not), we are drawn together in our loss of self (*Inner Experience*, 96; *OC* V, 113), and despite the relief that laughter represents once we are able to process it, it still represents a transmission of the sacred (as that which is beyond the individual) at a particular moment (98; 115).[7] Bataille also argues that to get beyond the self can entail either a loss between beings, or between a being and 'the beyond of being[s]' (*Guilty*, 139; *OC* V, 388, trans. mod.).

Either of these would be an ecstatic being, one that existed in a process, rather than just being a transcended subject/individual, as 'ecstasy is, it seems, communication' (*Inner Experience*, 12; *OC* V, 24). Communication is an extension of the process of 'contagion', and the reason why it maintains this threatening quality is that we

In sacrifice we also have consumption, and 'consumption is the way in which *separate* beings communicate' (*The Accursed Share*, 58; *OC* VII, 63). This communication is to be the opening of ourselves, such that 'everything is open and infinite between those who consume intensely' (ibid.). Bataille goes on to state that the society that forms or *persists* around this is not to be totally rejected, as excess needs the cumulative aspect, and the latter, as the 'everyday form of community', can be more or less amenable to the irruption of the other type.

Once again there are complications, as essentially, for Bataille, one form of existence (being open to and in excess) is real, and the mundane one of work, profit and accumulation is wrong. He goes so far as to say that human existence is communication (in his sense of the word) or it is not really human existence: 'communication is not at all something additional to human reality, but constitutive of it' (*Inner Experience*, 24; *OC* V, 37), so that 'the various separate(d) beings *communicate*, come to life, in losing themselves in the *communication* between one another' (*Guilty*, 27; *OC* V, 263, trans. mod.). This communication consists of eroticism, as well as sacrifice, laughter, drunkenness, and so on – and also includes the notion of laying bare oneself before another (so not always literally erotic). In a clear statement linking communication and sacrifice, Bataille shows us how his terms are linked, without them saying quite the same thing (note also the explicit questioning of the possible truth of the terms): 'It is important for me to show that in "communication", in love, desire has the void [le néant] as its object. This is how it is in all "sacrifice"' (*On Nietzsche*, 20; *OC* VI, 44, trans. mod.).

Communication, then, is arguably a concept that underpins much, if not all, of Bataille's theorizations, but its particular site as a term is in *Inner Experience* and *Guilty*. Like Derrida after him, Bataille is not content to let terms become accumulations of meaning, so that they can be easily defined. Already we have seen a shifting between sacrifice, the sacred, contagion and communication. Before passing on to 'continuity', there is a further relevant term that features in *The Accursed Share*. This term is intimacy, and it signals the return (to be completed in *Eroticism*) to an erotically charged way of describing a process that occurs everywhere (as in 'Solar Anus').

Intimacy is the link between us that is restored through sacrifice – and it is significant that the idea of return is a feature of the use of 'intimacy'. Bataille writes that in sacrifice, 'man is *in search of a lost intimacy* from the first' (*The Accursed Share*, 57; *OC* VII, 62). The awareness Bataille has of nostalgia counters claims that he himself is nostalgic for a return to a true order where we all communicate freely (even if he often asserts something of this nature), because it is clear that what was lost *was and is always lost*, as it is never attainable).[10] Consumption and putting oneself at risk are ways of being intimate (58; 63). In modern society we are not to resort to a second level nostalgia, but the way is open for a different form of intimacy. This is because the dominance of the bourgeois, profane, restricted order has undone the old religions, which themselves sought to control, if not destroy, the sacred (Bataille writes of religions as being only an 'external form of intimacy' 129; 123). This bourgeois order has also removed, in Protestantism and Rationality, any (external) foundations for its claim to be true. Once all bases for truth are removed, we have the 'world of things' on one hand and, in a way, more of a chance of acceding to, if not capturing, or living, the sacred. This sacred is now in the form of a 'pure intimacy' (189; 178), if it *is* at all – a sacred of nothingness, or perhaps NOTHING, that presumably is approachable though 'profane' means such as eroticism.

Eroticism opens with a discussion of the distinction between 'discontinuous individuals' (12; *OC* X, 18) and continuity of being. The latter is where it all begins. For Bataille, creatures such as the amoeba live in a state of continuous being – that is, there is nothing

Death and continuity emerge in the sacrifice, where the victim is merged with the continuity beyond us, and in this, we are dragged out of ourselves as well (see 82, 86–7; 84, 87–9). Now that we can see that Bataille maintains this over many texts and years of writing, we can ask, 'Do we all have the same relation in sacrifice?' The simplistic answer is that the sacrificer has the power, and benefits most. Then there are two alternatives, according to how far we accept the notion of contagion: we are all brought fully in to the sacrifice through contagion; or it is the 'victim' who actually encounters the sacred, with the rest going part of the way. Perhaps all three models are possible, with the most 'successful' being the occasions where contagion comes into play.

We fear losing ourselves in eroticism, or in drunkenness. This fear of loss of self in an other is potentially a masculinist perception, but we can allow that, for Bataille, the fear is to be welcomed, not overcome, avoided or destroyed – for example he states that 'bodies open out to a state of continuity' (17; 23), and this is the height of experience, with the dread of loss of self a product of the 'restricted', everyday world. In eroticism itself (as opposed to sex, which is the functional version – i.e. in the pursuit of reproduction) we come together in *loss*, not unity – what is between us is nothing:

> At the moment of conjunction the animal couple is not made up of two discontinuous beings drawing close together uniting in a current of momentary continuity: there is no real union; two individuals in the grip of violence brought together by the preordained reflexes of sexual intercourse share in a state of crisis in which both are beside themselves. Both creatures are simultaneously open to continuity. (103; 103–4)[12]

Community, then, is not just in the loss of self, but in the coming together of individuals lost to subjectivity. Not for Bataille the supposed empathy of the drug Ecstasy, as we do not 'become one' – we seem more likely to become none. This nothing is continuity or death, and can spread, in, for example, the orgies of the Bacchae or maenads (*Eroticism*, 113; *OC* X, 114).[13] The orgy is a useful figure to end on, as it is a form of 'fête', involving transgression and eroticism, and is potentially ridiculous. In concluding this chapter, we can work back from the notions of continuity, communication and so on to see them already 'prefigured' in an episode in a much earlier text.

In 'The Pineal Eye', we see a fine example of a sacrificial gathering, and one that highlights something I have not thus far brought out – the way in which sacrifice can be written, so as to be itself sacrificial. For Bataille, this entails the total involvement of the writer (as opposed to objective discourse), along with elements of shock, and also, crucially, risibility as a vital part of the excess. Risibility requires the lowering of the self, as 'man, in acts of the flesh, breaks free, in dirtying, in dirtying himself, from the limit of being(s)' (*On Nietzsche*, 22; *OC* VI, 45, trans. mod.). Note how demanding this position is: one must not only lower oneself into what one dreads as dirty and impure, in order both to be at the 'summit of being' and to show the ridiculousness of such a posture or belief, one must also be conscious of the stupidity of the whole project – there is no sense that to reach total degradation is a triumph.[14]

In the section 'The Sacrifice of the Gibbon', of 'The Pineal Eye'(85– 6; *OC* II, 28–30), such sovereign risibility occurs. The scene centres on a gibbon, who is to be buried alive, and an Englishwoman (as the epitome of upright morals, like Sir Edmund in *The Story of the Eye*) who leads the proceedings, and who loses herself in the process. Once tied up to a stake in a pit, the gibbon's 'bestially howling mouth swallows dirt whole, on the other end, her huge screaming pink anal protrusion stares at the sky like a flower' ('The Pineal Eye', 85; *OC* II, 29). The people around the pit, naked and increasingly excited by the spectacle, shovel dirt in. The rear end is left exposed:

overtakes the sordid humans, who become part of a celebration beyond them:

> The sun vomited like a sick drunk above the mouths full of comic screams, in the void of an absurd sky. . . . And thus an unparalleled heat and stupor formed an alliance [. . .] and celebrated a wedding [. . .], the little copulation of the stinking hole with the sun . . . (86; 30)

Notes

1. Bataille refers to this himself in *Lascaux*, but draws the line differently in that text, arguing that humanity can be distinguished through its capacity for art (which he further distinguishes from art in the sense of tool-making, and technical skills).

2. See 'Sacred Sociology and the Relationships between "Society", "Organism", and "Being"'.

3. This community with Nietzsche is fleshed out in *Somma Atheologica* (*Inner Experience*, 25–7; *OC* V, 38–40 and extensively in *On Nietzsche*). In the latter of these texts, the closing volume of the *Somma Atheologica*, Bataille pursues the question of inner experience through the writings of Nietzsche, in addition to the 'mystical experiences' of sex, drunkenness and so on. As Nietzsche opens up the possibility of community, Bataille wishes to extend it: 'My life, in the company of Nietzsche, is a community, my book is this community' (*On Nietzsche*, 9; *OC* VI, 33 trans. mod.). Or, as in another celebrated text, 'my name is legion. . .'

4. Bataille's sacred is close to Walter Benjamin's conception of aura ('The Work of Art in the Era of Mechanical Reproduction'). For Benjamin, 'the essentially distant object is the unapproachable one. Unapproachability is indeed a major quality of the cult image. True to its nature, it remains "distant, however close it may be"'('The Work of Art', 236–7n.).

5. Many writers who would be seen as parallel to Bataille have emphasized that the sacred is what must be separated off, and maintained at a distance: Durkheim, René Girard (*Violence and the Sacred* and *The Scapegoat*), Henri Hubert and Marcel Mauss (*Sacrifice*), Mary Douglas (*Purity and Danger*). Perhaps the closest to Bataille's view is that presented by Kristeva in *Powers of Horror*. For Bataille, this separation never goes away, but it does dissolve at particular moments of 'violent silence'.

6. Bataille can be more firm in his affirmation of the difference between what is sacred and what is transcendent: 'the sacred is exactly the opposite of transcendence' ('Le Mal dans le platonisme et dans le sadisme' ('Evil in Platonism and in Sadism') (*OC* VII, 369).

7. See also 'La Limite de l'utile' ('The Limit of the Useful'), *OC* VII, 181–280, and *Guilty*, 101– 8; *OC* V, 346–55. It is worth noting that although the *Somma Atheologica* and *The Accursed Share* can be seen as parallel, separate systems, close inspection of the notes and drafts from the 1940s suggests a continual attempt to merge the systems. Typically enough, this merging comes not at a moment of truth, but at

moments of loss, such as in the contagion of group laughter, based on the sacrifice of the person being laughed at. There is also a parallel with Antonin Artaud's notion of 'theatre as plague' in *The Theatre and its Double*, 7–22.

8. See also 'Schéma d'une histoire des religions'('Outline of a History of Religions') , *OC* VII, 406–42, where Bataille mentions that in sacrifice 'there is simply a void that is open and [a void] across which a sacred communication takes place' (417).

9. As Bataille notes in an earlier text, 'Sacrificial Mutilation and the Severed Ear of Van Gogh', certain artists show the persistence of a notion of the sacred as violent intervention that is yet relevant to and comprehensible (in a way) to society. The question of the sovereign writer, particularly in the form of Nietzsche, parallels this conception. Such writers or artists can create a sense, if that is the right word, of the sacred through their attempts to get beyond themselves into a communal loss (i.e. between their art and the viewer/reader).

10. He emphasizes that sacrifice is nostalgic, in the fully melancholic sense, with sacrifice being 'the nostalgia for a glory which only truly belongs to the heavens' ('La Limite de l'utile', *OC* VII, 189).

11. See also the brilliantly titled section, 'Sexual Plethora and Death' (*Eroticism*, 94–108; *OC* X, 95–109).

12. In addition to the masculinist posture of Bataille, it is always assumed by Bataille that sex is heterosexual, *even if his theories suggest no such thing*.

13. This loss of self is suggestive of a masculinist philosophy. But here we have the examples of maenads and Bacchae, and Blanchot, while discussing Bataille, uses Marguerite Duras exemplary of such a conception of eroticism ('The Community of Lovers', *The Unavowable Community*, 29–56).

14. Bataille also links love, crime and dirt: 'so "communication" – without which, for us, nothing would be – is assured by crime. "Communication" is love, and love soils all those it unites' (*On Nietzsche*, 18; *OC* VI, 43 trans. mod.). The link between dirt and love should not be seen just as a fear or disavowal of love – dirt and dirtying (*souillure*) are to do with breaking seemingly fixed barriers – between people, and through the transgression of rules – of which, more in the next chapter.

15. As is all too common with Bataille in his use of erotic imagery in his art,

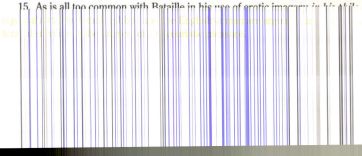

6

Eroticism and Transgression

In a sense, Bataille's thought on eroticism flows directly from his writings on community, whether in terms of losing the self in the other, or in the more precise term – continuity – he proposes for such a phenomenon. Sex and eroticism have featured from the start of Bataille's writings, whether in 'theory' like 'Solar Anus', or in fiction such as *The Story of the Eye*. Eroticism is central to the general economy (as are death, waste, expenditure, laughter, drunkenness), particularly in *The Accursed Share*, vol. II (*The History of Eroticism*), but it has always been part of something more than sex, and has always been to do with cycles of life and death:

> Disasters, revolutions, and volcanoes do not make love with the stars. The erotic revolutionary and volcanic deflagrations antagonize the heavens. As in the case of violent love, they take place beyond the constraints of fecundity. [. . .]Love, then, screams in my own throat; I am the Jesuve, the filthy parody of the torrid and blinding sun.
>
> I want to have my throat slashed while violating the girl to whom I will have been able to say: you are the night. ('Solar Anus', 8–9; *OC* I, 86)

Even in this early text, all of the essential elements of eroticism are in place: reproductive sex is merely animal – there must be more for it to be eroticism; eroticism is inseparable from death; eroticism is ridiculous *at the same time* as it gets beyond the everyday; finally, and all too often, it is about a gendered subjectivity (and loss of same), where women are means to ends – something supposedly surpassed in Bataille's thought.

So, eroticism is part of the general thought of Bataille, but has a clear focus in *Eroticism*, which reiterates much of the as then unpublished second volume of *The Accursed Share*, but does so in a way that is more insistent on the specificity of eroticism. As well as developing the idea of 'continuity', *Eroticism* is where we see the most detailed articulation of a notion of transgression. The book stands midway between the valorizations of sexual liberation offered by surrealism (and later by writers such as Marcuse, and, arguably, Deleuze and Guattari) and the bleaker views of Foucault, whose essay 'Preface to Transgression' is one of the earliest major essays on Bataille, and central to Foucault's work.

For Bataille, there is no possible sexual liberation, even if psychoanalysis offers something of the sort (*OC* X, 631n.). He criticizes the surrealists for thinking Sade to be an advocate of it (*Eroticism*, 183; *OC* X, 182), arguing insistently that what is important with Sade is to maintain the sense of horror. Bataille's novels do not offer any resolution, any conventional release. Instead, they centre on death, degradation and risible events, often of a sexual nature. In fact, we might ask whether he is even interested in sex as such (the same question can be asked of Sade). Following this path takes us to another influential follower of Bataille (at least in one book) – Kristeva, whose *Powers of Horror* builds on Bataille's notion of abjection. So, while we might think there is a loss of sexualized identity in sexual liberation, we are also left with a curious discrepancy between a notion of loss of self and a notion of one perhaps resolved in a notion of radically excessive sexuality in Bataille.

death, loss of the self), Bataille opens up the erotic as both deadly and where life actually is at its height. Eroticism is 'assenting to life up to the point of death' (*Eroticism*, 11; *OC* X, 17) and 'in essence, the domain of eroticism is the domain of violence, of violation' (16; 22). In order, then, to 'live life to the full', death (in the form of loss of the self) must be encountered (but not overcome or mastered). The individual must be threatened with their own dissolution, and this is what is meant by eroticism being about violation. Nakedness – literal and metaphorical – offers an early glimpse of what might be at stake, and emphasizes that eroticism is not about individualistic practice, or self-fulfilment:

> Stripping naked is the decisive action. Nakedness offers a contrast to self-possession, to discontinuous existence, in other words. It is a state of communication revealing a quest for a possible continuance of being beyond the confines of the self. Bodies open out to a state of continuity through secret channels that give us a feeling of obscenity. The term obscenity signifies that which disrupts the physical state associated with self-possession. (17; 23 trans. mod.)

Nakedness is an opening of the self such that the self, in going over to the other, becomes other, becomes something it normally is not allowed to be. The question of norms, taboos, conventions and so on recurs throughout *Eroticism*, but it is already clear here that obscenity is not a term containing a negative value judgement. Rather it is what is *deemed* to be obscene. Note that instead of overcoming this by advocating that all should be permitted, it is the obscenity that is important in its own right, and this is because what is forbidden is precisely what is more relevant, in terms of sovereign existence.

Sovereign existence is fundamentally tied to the originary (i.e. admittedly speculative and ultimately unfindable) moment that 'we' became human. Sovereignty is the highest possibility, but also tends to feature what we, in the normal run of things, exclude as fearful, dangerous and so on. Eroticism as much as death (and our awareness of it) is this originary moment, as eroticism, being more than animal sex, must include our becoming aware of sex as something other than a natural function (even if to think 'natural function' is already to require us to no longer be 'natural'). Once again, we have one of Bataille's paradoxical conceptions: eroticism is both our 'coming to humanity', and the loss of this humanity (as we step, or more accurately, fall, outside it). Eroticism, like sovereignty, is a process of conscious self-loss (perhaps in the belief of self-fulfilment) that brings with it an actual loss of self, an excess or exceeding of self (*Eroticism*, 31; *OC* X, 35). Eroticism is precisely not the norm, normal, or to be normalized (170; 169), it cannot be known – any attempt to master eroticism, to 'make it good', merely brings it into the realm of a restricted economy of sex and sexuality.[1] At many points, then, in *Eroticism* (and in *The Tears of Eros*), it seems as if the separation of the erotic constitutes part of our 'essential humanity', in the same way as the separation of the sacred or awareness of death. But in *Eroticism* Bataille is quick to point out that, for him, it is *work* that sets humanity apart, sets it up.

Work features in the awareness of death, in that we acquire an awareness of life as linear, as something approaching a project, and thus acquire a sense of duration (see *Eroticism*, 30–1; *OC* X, 34–5). In order to counter 'the ravages of time', we work, believe in projects, and thereby distance the 'beyond' from us: death is increasingly kept away. The sacred and eroticism are part of the same process: they are not just pure threats, but are seen as threats *because they threaten the world of work*, i.e. the putative restricted economy. It must be stressed that the question of 'which came first' is raised by Bataille only to render the situation more paradoxical: the origin might be in work and the profane world, but the existence of that world is as much a result of what is inside us, and our inside a result of the 'outside' (this perpetual shifting, even

his discussion of prehistoric cave paintings, Bataille remarks on the 'coincidence of death and eroticism' (ibid.). It is as if taboos could exist without there actually being a moral component, something we might find hard to follow from our perspective, which emerges from a society that systematizes itself in a moralistic fashion.[2]

Taboos are, however, linked to the sacred, at an overt level, in terms of what is holy, what is unholy and what is profane, and at the level on which Bataille wishes to address the sacred, which is to do with what kind of a thing the sacred is: that which is outside, or to be kept outside. Hence the following statements on taboo:

> It is ridiculous to isolate a specific 'taboo' such as the one on incest, just one aspect of the general taboo, and look for its explanation outside its universal basis, namely the amorphous and universal prohibitions bearing on sexuality. [. . .] This amorphous and universal taboo is constant. Its shape and its object do change; but whether it is a question of sexuality or death, violence, terrifying yet fascinating, is what it is levelled at. (*Eroticism*, 50–1; *OC* X, 53–4)

Taboo then is universal, but *as* taboo, not as any specific one (even if elsewhere, such as in *The Accursed Share*, vol. II, Bataille does suggest that the existence of taboos around the dead, if of varying types, perhaps, is in itself universal). Taboo is a defence mechanism, but also creates a space for what is to be defended against. In this Bataille once again 'recalls' Foucault, who in *Discipline and Punish* argues that crime is actually constructed by the legal and penal systems (for example, certain drugs come to be illegal, thereby creating new criminals). So taboo aims both to reduce our fear and to maintain it, and this is what is so fascinating in taboo, and in what is taboo: seeing a dead body is arguably only fearful once the idea of death as something fearful is in place, and then only really when this fear is not allowed to occur, as in contemporary Western societies.[3]

Taboo is the refusal of nature, and the establishing of nature as something to be refused, controlled and so on (*Eroticism*, 61–2; *OC* X, 64–5). Included in this is the distancing of women and the feminine, via the taboos on menstruation (53–4; 56–7). All that is rejected or distanced is part of the sacred, and can be recalled, at moments, through processes that parallel sacrifice – essentially, here at least, uncontrolled eroticism. This recall takes the form of transgression, which is absolutely part of taboo, as it 'suspends a taboo without suppressing it' (36; 39).

Transgression is a possibility contained within taboo – or else there would be no need for the taboo. Similarly, there is nothing that is inherently transgressive (and therefore inherently evil) – transgression requires taboo ('evil is not transgression, it is transgression condemned'[127; 127]). What is at stake, then, is more than simply breaking a rule – it is the replaying of the fact of having rules, and of there being an outside to them. As this in some way figures as a recall of 'the origin' (the only time the origin exists?), it must entail consciousness, only this time it entails loss of conscious control, mastery, Reason, or any end beyond the moment. Transgression is intentional (90; 91) and passes through 'consciousness of the void' (69; 72), which is then lost in 'exaltation' (ibid.). At this stage we are approaching the 'pinnacle of being' (276; 270), as in sovereignty – i.e. the highpoint is also the falling away, the loss of self.

Transgression could logically be applied to much of Bataille's writing, in terms of its approach, in terms of the specific notions that occur – but transgression is not the province of the individual. Even if it is the individual acting alone, transgression, like sovereignty, can only occur with the loss of the self in the other, whether this other be 'the void', someone else or a sacrificial community. Transgression is also allocated sites where it can occur, where the taboo is lifted (*not* broken), in order perhaps to better control what is fearful, seen as dangerous. I will deal with two specific examples killing; both are a sanctioned breaking of the taboo on killing (the saying 'all's fair in love and war' is stating that elsewhere this is not the case). The death penalty, on the other hand, is purely rationalistic, and even Sade, a great lover of inflicting death (in literature), is against it.[5]

The other significant, and perhaps puzzling, example is that of sex in marriage as transgression, as it relates to marriage. In terms of transgressing the rules of marriage, there is firstly some version of the incest taboo, based on the exchange of women (*Eroticism*, 197–222; *OC* X, 196–217), which defines who can marry, who can have sex, and with whom. Secondly, we would then see some further restriction or rule as a result of the completion of something resembling marriage. By combining the above, transgression would *become* the disobeying of these restrictions – having sex with someone you should not, or having sex in a way one should not (hence in some Western countries it is heterosexual sodomy that is illegal). Bataille, however, would have it that all eroticism (in this instance, sex of some sort other than reproductive) remains 'taboo' – transgression, in other words, and marriage is the sanctioned breaking of this taboo, and not the place where the taboo does not apply: 'hence just as killing is simultaneously forbidden and performed in sacrificial ritual, so the initial sexual act constituting marriage is a permitted violation' (109; 110–11).

It applies particularly, but not only, to the initial sexual act, which is 'more' of a transgression, especially if a virgin is involved, notes Bataille (and clearly the woman is meant by this, as the taboo being broken is of 'penetration' by a stranger). In the long term, sex in marriage is transgression, as it is sex with a close relative. This last of Bataille's arguments about marriage is the strangest, since if transgression is what is deemed by a society not to be permissible, then this is certainly not the case with many societies' view of marriage – furthermore, what about systems where sex with the spouse exists not for pleasure but for procreation (where sex would be utilitarian and *limited*)? Sex within marriage would be linked with transgression as the possibility of breaking the taboo, by having 'sex outside marriage' (sex outside the *terms* of marriage) and encountering the line of demarcation (111; 112). Not only that, but, according to Bataille, very often the creation of habit between sexual partners allows more, not less, likelihood of eroticism, whereas 'casual sex' is more likely to be animal sex (ibid.). We can perhaps summarize the contradictory possibilities in saying that marriage is the site around which eroticism as taboo/transgression occurs and that all eroticism exists against the 'permissions' or 'restrictions' of marriage, but cannot exist independently of such rules.

More consistently with what we know of the rest of his philosophy, Bataille then writes of orgies and the 'contagion' that is their essence, and I wish to raise this point with reference to what he says about prostitution, to highlight the discrepancy between an active feminine (or female) excessive eroticism, and a rendering of women as objects. He writes, about the maenads, archetypical female Dionysians, that 'orgiacal eroticism is by nature a dangerous excess whose explosive contagion is an indiscriminate threat to all sides of life' (113; 114). In contrast to these women who can access subjectivity and its loss, prostitutes are objects of excess. In talking of the 'erotic object' (130; 130), he specifies first that it could be male or female, but then continues:

> but with [women's] passive attitude they try by exciting desire to bring about the conjunction that men achieve by pursuing them. They are no more desirable, but they lay themselves open to be desired.
>
> They put themselves forward as objects for the aggressive desire of men. Not every woman is a potential prostitute, but prostitution is the logical consequence of the feminine attitude. (131; 130–1)

These statements are by no means an essential part of the theory, but the regularity with which they appear suggest they are an essential part of Bataille's writing. The evidence for the inappro-

and who will never pass by subjectivity. This distinction is far less certain in Bataille's fiction, to which we now turn.

Anguish and Apathy

As with many of Bataille's notions, eroticism cannot be separated from an experience which keeps it at bay while it is simultaneously being pursued. This experience, which opens up onto 'inner experience', is the experiencing of anguish, as our discontinuous being is revealed as such and *as part of continuity – i.e. death and eroticism*. Much of his writing on 'inner experience' emphasizes this aspect – hence the importance of heightened, rather than pleasurable, states (and the latter includes standard mystical states which seek to attain something, even if this something is 'nothing'). *Guilty*, can be seen as an account of living the perverse arbitrariness of existence – and how this is to be done in the form of an irredeemable guilt. The continued reappearance of the pictures of the Chinese man being tortured, and their final, literal, appearance in *The Tears of Eros*, constitutes a privileged site of the occurrence of anguish as a form, or precursor, of ecstasy. In *Eroticism* this anguish is presented as occurring in the formation of taboos, but also at moments when they are at issue – where the taboo is threatened, such as in sacrifice, or in erotic acts (themselves a form of sacrificial community):

> If we observe the taboo, if we submit to it, we are no longer conscious of it. But in the act of violating it we feel the anguish of mind without which the taboo could not exist: that is the experience of sin. That experience leads to the completed transgression, the successful transgression which, in maintaining the prohibition, maintains it in order *to benefit by it. The inner experience of eroticism demands from the subject a sensitiveness to the anguish of taboo no less great than the desire which leads him to infringe it*. (*Eroticism*, 38–9; *OC* X, 42)

Anguish is essential, and signals the fact that transgression is failure: failure of the self either to *be* or to get beyond the self, and this failure is transgression. So far, it seems logical that anguish comes after the establishing of the prohibition (although causality is impossible to determine: why ban something if it is not frightening? how or why should we be frightened of something before we have a system of thinking to tell us to be frightened?), and before any 'transgressive acts'. Bataille expands, however, arguing that after having lived sovereignly at some fleeting moment, we are left with a wound, and further anguish:

> In human life, on the other hand, sexual violence causes a wound that rarely heals of its own accord; it has to be closed, and even without the constant attention based on anguish, it cannot remain closed. Primary anguish bound up with sexual disturbance signifies death. The violence of this disturbance reopens, in the mind of the man experiencing it, who knows what death is, the abyss that death once revealed. (104; 105 trans. mod.)

Anguish is important, but Bataille is far from recommending the Christian fear of sexual matters; he is trying to identify how it came about and in what way it is positive (in the sense of being *productive* of something). Is he, though, recommending some form of overcoming of the fear and anguish? In a temporary, unassimilable way, the answer would have to be yes, for in moments of sovereignty, within eroticism, for an instant, there would be no one to be anguished. These moments beyond anguish (or are they *in* anguish?) leave their mark, nonetheless, and certainly much of the fiction is preoccupied with fear, worry, guilt, anguish, embarrassment, and an embrace of degradation for its own sake. But there is another way of experiencing eroticism, one that seems to apply more to Sade than to Bataille's own fictions, ostensibly at least, and this other possibility is apathy.

According to Bataille, Sade's system, at its most comprehen-

This apathy leads them to leave behind the inane joys of pleasure, which are only a calming down of excess, a control, and instead to pursue what threatens this apathy. So, in other words, apathy is not a goal in itself either – if it were, then Bataille would have been arguing in favour of Protestantism and capitalism. Apathy is only of interest if at the height of sovereignty – always open to the possibility, even if it is negligible, of being exceeded. And of course the apathy of the fiction is not necessarily to be replicated in the reader. A classic example of this would be Bret Easton Ellis's *American Psycho*, wherein the central character mutilates and kills a succession of women, in between shopping, snorting cocaine and so on. The apathy is not without the risk of inspiring a similar apathy. Neither is it without the risk of attracting highly non-apathetic reactions of outrage.

Not everyone in such novels is equally apathetic. Sade's Justine fascinates the 'libertines' because she simply cannot lose her moral views, no matter what happens. Similarly, killing apathetic victims will inspire only boredom among the already apathetic. In Bataille's fiction I think we see an element of this apathy, and more particularly at the textual, stylistic, level, where the anguish of participants is rendered 'flatly'. In his fiction we see a continual dialogue, or dynamic, between anguish and apathy, with eroticism providing the 'organizing' moments.

Stories of Excess

The Story of the Eye follows the escalating exploration of eroticism by the unnamed (male) narrator and his friend Simone. Starting with Simone lowering herself onto a bowl of milk for the cat, and the narrator watching, it ends with a sadistic and blasphemous scene centred on the erotic murder of a priest in his church. Along the way, another two characters are involved: Marcelle and Sir Edmund. The first of these perhaps represents repressed sexuality – her first experience of orgasm (at least within the book) is when she has locked herself into a cupboard while an orgy is going on, and is complete only when she urinates. She, like the two protagonists, is obsessed with fluids, especially bodily ones, but never overcomes her anguish around eroticism; eventually she hangs herself, after the narrator and Simone have helped her escape from an asylum where she had kept herself amused by frequent urination, and presumably masturbation. Sir Edmund is a very different type of caricature – the seedy side of the apparently upright British aristocracy. He assists the two in their projects, and seems to function as a benevolent, if lascivious, uncle.

Barthes traces another narrative, pursuing a chain of metaphors, and arguing for the metonymic nature of *The Story of the Eye* ('The Metaphor of the Eye', 125). This is largely based on the similarity in French between eye and egg: *des yeux* and *des œufs*, which leads Bataille, through Simone, to posit the similarity in terms of the objects. Simone also pursues this in terms of balls (we also hear of 'castrated eyes' [42; *OC* I, 45 trans. mod.]), eventually eating bull's balls (53; 56) and placing the dead priest's eye in her vulva (67; 69).

This is one of the more obvious elements in the story, it is true, but it is more interesting to wonder at how metaphor *as a function* breaks down.[6] In terms of what the characters do, there is no more metaphor: everything is to be done 'literally'. At another level we could also pursue the 'metaphors' of liquidity that pervade the novel – something which in itself suggests an attack on the simple split that allows metaphor to stand, untroubled, for something else. In one short passage alone we see 'raindrops', 'the sea', 'legs wet with come', 'hot rain [. . .] pouring down and streaming', 'a mud puddle', 'smearing herself', 'downpour', 'soil-covered', 'wallowing in the puddle' (12–13; 16–17). Liquid takes the participants beyond themselves 'morally', physically, erotically – into the continuity that will appear in *Eroticism*.

> I drew [Simone's] thighs apart, and found myself facing something I imagine I had been waiting for in the same way that a guillotine waits for a neck to cut. I even felt as if my eyes were bulging from my head, erectile with horror; in *Simone*'s hairy vagina, I saw the pale blue eye of *Marcelle*, gazing at me, crying tears of urine. Streaks of come in the steaming hair helped give that dreamlike vision a disastrous sadness. (67; 69 trans. mod.)

The narrator is the guillotine – apathetic in his waiting to cut, not fearful of castration, but not because castration has been overcome. The eye here is of the priest, but the continuity of death summons Marcelle (who has also been invoked at another point, as we will shortly see). This evocation does inspire fear, nonetheless, and feasibly eyes 'erectile with horror' risk being plucked out – but it is the irruption of death (and/or erotic continuity) which brings anguish, an anguish that is not for a particular organ or symbol, but for the border of all continuity. This continuity is not reducible to a castration complex, as such a complex is within the reduction to 'restricted economy' that is being left behind (the 'castrated eyes' above refer to the state of normal society, not something that might occur, and would therefore be fearfully awaited). Not escaped, just rendered irrelevant. And because, like all closed systems, psycho-analysis has an answer for all contingencies, this is where it can 'trap' Bataille's fiction – in attempting to dissolve boundaries and so on, through eroticism/death, it is arguably avoiding the question, or, better still, making a fetish of it.[7]

Much more important than the above is the role of dirt, of dirty-ing (*souillure*). Dirt breaks down the barriers between individuals, between individuals and their morals, and breaks down the codes of society as it breaks with the discontinuity of individuals. Simone, from an early stage, is after *souillure*. She pisses on him, then he takes his turn. He then comes on her face, at which point, 'dirtied all over she began to come – a liberating frenzy' (21; 25 trans. mod.).[8] The narrator, too, loves all that is to do with dirt:

> I did not care for what are known as 'pleasures of the flesh' because in truth they are always insipid [. . .]. My kind of debauchery soils not only my body and thoughts, but also anything I may conceive in its course, that is the vast starry universe, which merely serves as a back-drop. (42; 45)

Here we see the general economy where all can be brought together *in coming apart*. Death plays a crucial part in all of Bataille's writing, but what is interesting here is that death itself seems totally subsumed into erotic possibilities. What is normally to be feared (death, dirt) is still feared, is maintained as fearful, but a form of apathy comes in as to the outcome, and there is no after-effect as a result of death or 'pollution' (e.g. guilt).

The first death in the book is taken lightly, and fuels Simone and the narrator's general curiosity, rather than specifically their interest in death. They knock over a cyclist, who dies, and 'the horror and despair at so much bloody flesh, nauseating in part, and in part very beautiful, was fairly equivalent to our usual impression on seeing one another' (11; 10). End of episode. Similarly, Marcelle's death stimulates an investigative, if eventually uncontrolled, exploration of her dead body. Through the narrator's 'boredom' and 'lack of excitement' (43; 46), he feels nearer to Marcelle, in her death.[9]

Which brings us to perhaps the defining moment in the narrative, where a bullfighter is gored while Simone deals with the balls of the previous bull. The narrator reflects on the moment:

> Two globes of equal size and consistency had suddenly been propelled in opposite directions at once. One, the white ball of the bull, had been thrust into the 'pink and dark' cunt that Simone had bared to the crowd; the other, a human eye, had spurted from Granero's head with the same force as a bundle of innards from a belly. This coincidence, tied to death and to a sort of urinary liquefaction of the sky, brought us, for the first time, close to *Marcelle*. (54; 57 trans. mod.)

Bataille's fiction is almost always concerned with the erotic, but is very rarely dealing with sex, nor is it written in a way that would encourage the same response as pornography. Susan Sontag points out (in 'The Pornographic Imagination') that there is a type of pornographic writing that works through sex and sexual response, in order to address something else, Bataille's writing being one example (and Pauline Réage's *The Story of O* another). For Bataille, eroticism is not opposed to sex; sex is the reduction of the erotic to something more manageable, controllable. His narrators, and/or protagonists are never far from ecstatic moments, but these are more likely to involve excretions of one sort or another than intercourse, or even more 'deviant' sexual practice, such as sadism or masochism. The wallowing in filth and the devotion often held by the male narrators toward female protagonists might well suggest a masochist economy, but freed of ritual and fixed fetishes.[10]

If one way of reading *The Story of the Eye* is to see it as a continuity of liquidity, then the same could be said of the fiction as a whole. The other links across the fictional texts are (usually) the presence of a central female character, and often moments of overt philosophizing, which, to be honest, work much less well than their understatement in *The Story of the Eye*. We would certainly be right to see a continuity between the fiction and philosophy, but the philosophical moments in the fiction are often heavy-handed.

Madame Edwarda is one of the more significant texts, as the eponymous woman, a prostitute, comes to stand for death and God. Bataille labours the point in a preface, but sections of the text are far more convincing in their own right, as when Madame Edwarda exposes herself: '"Why", I stammered in a subdued tone, "why are you doing that?" "You can see for yourself", she said, "I'm GOD"' (*Madame Edwarda*, 150; *OC* III, 20). The male narrator is doubly exposed to loss of meaning: firstly his own fear and puzzlement at his lack of knowledge, secondly GOD occurring in such a place (and perhaps thirdly, we have the masculinist reference to the vagina as a non-place, as GOD is NOTHING). The text goes on to describe the narrator putting his lips to this 'bared wound' (*Madame Edwarda*, 150; *OC* III, 20 trans. mod.). Passages such as this demonstrate the privileged position held by women by virtue of their sex. Women are nearer to the sacred, through their proximity to birth, but also to what is fearful. Now, what Bataille regards as privilege might not seem that way to everyone, but he is far from being misogynist – if anything, other than the hackneyed anguish at the sight of the 'absence' of genitals, it is the male actors who are the more abject, as they love absence, dirt and what is supposed to be fearful, and have little in the way of agency. Edwarda is perpetually beyond herself, through drunkenness, fever or sexual ecstasy. The narrator looks on, trying to work out why he is fascinated, and trying to find a meaning, as he pursues her impressive and willed loss of self. But there is to be no meaning, 'GOD' is only a pig, and all we have left is irony and the long wait for death (159; 30–1), so the narrator comes to occupy a 'low' sovereignty, wherein the search for truth, for what is ultimate, leads to nothing.

The Dead Man is a form of parable. Marie's husband dies and she is 'inspired' by this to go on a drunken debauch, recalling the killing of a king that unleashes the festival. Death pervades this story, and a demonic figure appears who may be the devil, or death. At the end this figure is cheated by Marie, who seems to die beyond his reach. Along the way there is much cause for public urination and other emanations, and the observation that sex is like the 'slaughtering of a pig or the laying to rest of a god' (188; *OC* IV, 47). Absurdity is once more at the heart of what otherwise would seem to be telling us an important truth. This story, unlike most of Bataille's, is fragmentary and highly obscure – elsewhere his style is knowingly minimal, consisting largely of dry observations.

Le Petit (*The Little One*) and *My Mother* are of interest at one

A lengthy exploration of these possibilities occurs in the shape of *My Mother*, but this time it is the mother who is active, the son-narrator the one to be led. How much is this just masochistic fantasy? It would be wrong to say there is no element of that in Bataille's fiction, but there are rarely rewards to be had – and the Bataillean narrator loses control, as opposed to relinquishing it on a temporary basis. If masochism there is, then it too, like sex, falls away in an ecstatic being that cannot know pleasure, cannot live pleasure.

Like *Madame Edwarda*, *My Mother* is intercut with slabs of portentous philosophical musing, but the story itself provides the points of (philosophical) interest. From the start, we know that Pierre, the son and narrator, and his mother, adore each other, whilst the narrator hates his father, whom he perceives as having mistreated his mother when he was alive. It eventually transpires that the relationship between father and mother was exactly the opposite, with the mother having countless affairs, getting drunk and so on. However, the narrator is the product of the father raping the mother. . . .

The mother loves all that is dirty, all that is forbidden. She tells the narrator that she is only at home in the mire (*My Mother*, 34; *OC* IV, 186), and that 'pleasure can only start when there is a worm in the fruit' (65; 216). Not only this, but she wants to take the narrator there too: 'I want to lead you into this world of death and corruption in which, as you begin to see, I am caught up' (133; 276 trans. mod.), and 'I want to bring you into my death' (ibid., trans. mod.). The story closes with the two about to consummate their relationship, with the mother declaring that afterwards she will die. Except that the act does not occur within the story – this would make it far too literal, far too much part of the world of standard desire, if outside the regulations. Also, along the way, there have been surrogates, who have had sexual relations with both the narrator and the mother.

In *My Mother* there is little of the cool description we see elsewhere; instead we have the oscillation of anguish and love the narrator feels for his mother, and a fairly straightforward narrative of initiation into perversity. The two remaining novel-length works, *The Blue of Noon* and *L'Abbé C*, focus on dirt, and the descent into anguish that propels and is brought on by proximity to *souillure*. *The Blue of Noon* features several women, who, in varying degrees, have or acquire a 'close relation' to what is 'low'. The most interesting is Dorothea, also known as Dirty. She has a strange combination of strength and the capacity to lose herself in excess. The narrator, Troppmann, goes along with her, but once more is definitely the follower. On the other hand, he is the instigator of debauchery with another woman, Xénie. The story has the coming war in Spain hovering in the background, the deathly counterpart to the embracing of death and dirt of the main characters (brought to a close by sex in a graveyard, with war about to come). Dirty is very close to sovereign in this book, in that she aspires to total subjectivity, through excess, and ultimately fails – a sovereign failure.

Perhaps perversely, *L'Abbé C* is very much a straightforward story, if framed in a way that problematizes its apparent simplicity (it is in the form of a diary, passed on to the 'author', who also writes certain of the sections). Within the 'content' there is also the issue of the twins, Robert and Charles, with the former as the 'abbot'. Essentially, the story revolves around Robert's loss of faith and eventual 'fall' into eroticism. Charles is happily engaged on the path of eroticism in any case. At the end, Robert is captured by the (collaborationist) police, and reveals the whereabouts of Charles and his lover, Éponine. So the figure of most significance in the novel moves from the heights of the priesthood, through a loss of faith and a desire to die and to experience the erotic (which he does), finishing in abject betrayal, *so that he can suffer from this betrayal in a perverse saintliness. Sovereignty comes to the lowest,* productive, issue of women's seeming proximity to the sacred, and this is the possibility of sovereignty, like death, being something that happens to someone else. It cannot happen to 'me', as the me cannot exist at the moment of sovereignty. So is it enough to witness sovereignty? Do the novels show sovereignty? If so, is it simply about content? Texts such as *Inner Experience*, and others from the same period, suggest that crossing of the borders of what is fiction, autobiography, philosophy etc., is important, but we should be wary of heading too quickly to one of two poles: the incorporation of the fiction into a *project* of self-realization; or an excitable reading of themes or styles taken in isolation.

Beyond Bataille's Fiction?

Bataille's fiction is strongly suggestive of a term that people attribute to Kristeva – 'abjection', which appears in *The Powers of Horror*. Abjection emerged in Chapter 2, above, in the context of death and horror. Here, via Kristeva (who opens *Powers of Horror* with an epigraph from Bataille's 'L'abjection et les formes misérables'), abjection is raised in terms of eroticism and the sexual identity of the individual. After 'abjection', there is an analysis of the related term of 'transgression', as it appears in Foucault's essay 'Preface to Transgression'.

Although Bataille focuses on the question of classes, and society's abjection as a whole, the phenomenon also applies to individuals (which is the aspect of primary importance to Kristeva). The question arises as to whether humans, or some humans, are inherently abject, or whether some things are inherently abject. Although Bataille certainly suggests the latter, this definition of how abjection comes about problematizes such ready categorization:

> the abjection of a human being is even negative in the formal sense, as it has an absence as its origin: it is merely the inability to assume with sufficient force the imperative act of excluding abject things (and that act establishes the foundations of collective existence). [. . .] So human abjection comes about as the result of the material incapacity to avoid contact with abject *things*: it is the abjection of *things*, communicated to those they touch. (*OC* II, 219)

In the first part of the quote above, we can see that abjection does not have a positive existence, and therefore, in principle, cannot be assumed through an act of will. The act of exclusion is necessary for collective existence, which exists (as in Bataille's writings on community) in the expulsion of what it fears, but in so doing fixes what is expelled as the danger. So society needs to distance death, dirt, eroticism and so on, but in distancing them only seems to shift the site of abjection. Abjection, then, becomes a given. In the second part, abjection seems much clearer – we can imagine contact with a corpse, or bodily fluids rendering the person abject. Being abject is also something 'material' – but we need to remember that Bataille's materialism is 'lower' than Marx's, which remains in the realms of concepts (i.e the economy). In the second part of the above quote, it seems as if some things are inherently abject, whilst in the first part, abjection seems to come from within. Bataille supplies a further comment, which maintains this paradox in a clearer way: 'the exclusion of what is rotten is constitutive of man' (*OC* II, 439n.).[11] This formulation allows an obscurity as to whether the chicken or the egg was abject first, as exclusion can be said to work retrospectively – i.e. it is the fact of being excluded rather than any inherent property of an 'abject thing' that leads to abjection as a condition.

Kristeva does not seek to resolve any of these paradoxes, but does try and account for the 'when' of abjection, and offers clearer statements of points raised by Bataille. For Kristeva, 'it is [thus] not lack of cleanliness or health that causes abjection but what dis-

about menstruation), but we get over it, and never know it happened. The 'abject individual', on the other hand, has this originary repression forcibly return. Much as in Bataille's notion of the sacred.

Kristeva goes on to argue that in order to live this abjection, the objects that create fear come to be associated with *jouissance*, eroticism. For her, this is a way of controlling them, or at least one that seems to be for the person she regards as a patient (9–10, 55). Similarly, individuals can live their abjection through writing – and Céline's anti-Semitism is taken as the archetypal, modern site of such writing (18, 140).[12] This is not a choice as such for the writers, but a manifestation of their abjection. Perhaps such a reading could be applied to Bataille – that he is unable to exclude what 'normal' people do, and therefore has to find an outlet for this. Even if this is the case, it still, whether in Kristeva or in Bataille's terms, indicates something which, for want of a better term, could be called 'the human condition'. Judith Still argues that we can take Bataille's fictional texts as 'a privileged example of what, for Kristeva, is a universal structure for all societies and all subjects, male and female' ('Horror in Kristeva and Bataille', 232–3).

Both writers would concur that modern society can only 'abject' through writing, or, perhaps, through social change. What does not seem possible is that we live 'abjection' (for it would not be seen as abject in the same way) through ritual, except in the case of something like 'obsessive-compulsive disorder'. At many levels, there is no escape either through, or in, abjection. Where that possibility seems to subsist is in the notion of transgression, and this should be seen as a notion that is parallel to abjection, even if Kristeva and Bataille differ on how they might coincide: 'certain aspects of the Bataillean text encourage a reading not as abject, but rather as heroic transgression, and Kristeva argues that transgression is a modality of *negation* whereas abjection is a question of *exclusion*' (Still, 'Horror in Kristeva and Bataille', 236n.).

One of the key essays on Bataille is Foucault's 'Preface to Transgression', which seeks to deal with both form and content of Bataille's writing, through the idea of (the possibility of) transgression. Like Derrida some years later, Foucault comes to the conclusion that the *writing* of transgression is the important thing, but along the way he raises the question of what exactly transgression is.

Transgression is ordinarily seen as the breaking of (a) law, or, the breaking of taboo. It is usually some form of extreme situation or behaviour. To transgress is to step outside the norm, and such stepping out requires punishment in order that the law holds. Transgression cannot, then, be separated from law, or notions of law – it is not in the act, but the illegality of an act that transgression lies. As Bataille writes, 'evil is not transgression, it is transgression condemned' (*Eroticism*, 127; *OC* X, 127), and this condemnation is the process whereby evil comes into existence. Similarly, if there were no transgressions, we would not need law – so law/taboo and transgression are bound up from the start, such that the origin of the distinction becomes unclear. But transgression is not simply doomed to fall within the boundaries of law, as it 'does not negate the taboo, but surpasses and completes it' (63; 63, trans. mod.). Transgression is both more and less than the breaking of a taboo or law – more because it goes beyond simple crime, less because it does not conclusively break or break with law/taboo.

In earlier societies the realm of taboo was clear – what was sacred was known and organized, and the transgression, in the form of the festival and/or sacrifice constituted the site of sanctioned transgression, but according to Foucault, modern society lives near to transgression; as it lives in the death of God. We now

together with prohibition, forms a unity which defines social life' (*Eroticism*, 65; *OC* X, 68, trans. mod.). At this stage it becomes less than clear whether transgression is really 'outside' of anything. Foucault writes that the line (law, taboo) that transgression crosses is always already crossed – i.e. the law is broken before it exists, and through its existence, whilst transgression is caught within law:

> Transgression, then, is not, finally, as black is to white, the prohibited to the permitted, the outside to the inside, the outcast to the sheltered space of the domicile. [. . .] Transgression does not oppose anything to anything, does not make anything slide in the play of derision, does not seek to disturb the solidity of foundations [. . .] it is the measure beyond measure of the distance that opens at the heart of the limit, and traces the flashing line that brings it into being. ('Preface to Transgression', 35 trans. mod.)

Foucault completes the thought of Bataille on this point, through a reading I would agree with, but that Bataille does not necessarily completely intend. There is plenty of evidence which suggests that transgression is a 'good thing' and, above all, that it is a choice. Bataille writes that 'eroticism, like cruelty, is premeditated. Cruelty and eroticism are conscious intentions in a mind taken with the resolution to trespass into a forbidden field of behaviour' (*Eroticism*, 79–80; *OC* X, 82 trans. mod.). Perhaps the way to unite the more voluntaristic version with the more ontological one is to say that they feed into each other so that the will to transgress is only a 'will' inspired by the existence of law, but once under way, transgression will be recalled as individuals lose themselves in sovereign moments.

Going back to Foucault, we see that sexuality might provide such a terrain, opening the way to eroticism in the '"real" sense', beyond sexuality. According to Foucault, we now define ourselves through sex, as opposed to with regard to God ('Preface to Transgression', 30–2, 50) – and in order to effect any alteration in our circumstances, we must address these areas where truth appears to hold. Furthermore, Bataille has managed to do this through writing, through crossing boundaries of types of writing, and through the strange content that accompanies the excessive way of writing. Going through the erotic, Bataille's language 'refers to itself and is folded back on a questioning of its limits' (44), and nowhere more so than in the upturned eye in *The Story of the Eye*. For Foucault, this eye shows the crossing between life and death, the possibility of reflection and its absence and so on – and instead of a philosophical text, the writing of transgression crosses into pornography (whilst the fiction hovers back into philosophy).

Arguably, the use of pornography as a genre subverts the criteria of philosophy, both in terms of content and in terms of reader-response. But some would raise the question of the validity of such an approach, arguing that 'philosophical porn' is the ultimate in male exploitative writing, allowing pornography into high culture. Bataille's attitude to women can often be as one-dimensional as the worst porn, though not in the pornographic writing, but in the philosophical texts. If I am honest, I have probably downplayed his perversely (because not theoretically consistent) misogynist moments.

Another definite criticism is his heterosexism – eroticism seems, bizarrely, to be almost invariably heterosexual (at least where the men are concerned – the mother of *My Mother* is almost exlusively lesbian), even if it rarely involves 'penetrative' sex. Bataille's protagonists might be polymorphously perverse, but maybe Butler's argument about homosexuality being excluded through abjection (in *Bodies That Matter*) could be applied to Bataille (it wouldn't, for example, be possible to apply it to Sade's fiction). Nonetheless, this has not stopped a 'queer' usage of Bataille, as in Sue Golding's 'Solar Clitoris', and if anything, Bataille .... to homosexual/lesbian writers such as William

128   *Georges Bataille*

the former there is an outside, which cannot be known, whilst for the latter (except for a few occasions), all 'outsides' exist only through their construction as discourse.

2. Incidentally, Bataille has a further alternative for the 'origin of humanity', also to do with these cave paintings. In *Lascaux* he argues that work might have started a process of humanization, but it is art, the capacity to imagine (i.e. not just the capacity to represent), which founds humanity (see *Lascaux*, *11*; *OC* IX, 11, and *passim*). Art also serves as something 'outside', akin to death and eroticism.

3. For a full development of this notion, building on Bataille, see Baudrillard, *Symbolic Exchange and Death*. See also Julian Pefanis, *Heterology and the Postmodern*, for further exegesis of the similarities between Bataille, Baudrillard and Lyotard.

4. Foucault writes, of this line: 'it is likely that transgression has its entire space in the line it crosses [. . .] transgression crosses and recrosses a line which closes up behind it' ('Preface to Transgression', 34).

5. For a classic example of just how rationalist this can be, we need only look at Rousseau, *The Social Contract* (Book 2, chapter 5), where Rousseau carefully limits the application of the death penalty, but when it is necessary, it is so because of the logical consistency of legitimate justice systems, and not due to the severity of particular crimes.

6. On this question, see also Sarah Kofman, *Nietzsche and Metaphor*. For Kofman, Bataille, like Nietzsche, raises the question of metaphoricity, with circularity, but in way that pre-empts the existence of discrete metaphors. Bataille (in 'Solar Anus') 'substitutes for the traditional hierarchy of concepts an indefinite circularity of terms with no hierarchy [. . .]. The circularity of the signifier mimics and, parodically, coincides with sexual circularity, which breaks with the opposition between high and low, masculine and feminine' (181n.). While this does not contradict Barthes, it suggests that his language is perhaps too caught up in literary criticism for him to notice the role he attributes to straightforward metaphor in Bataille.

7. There is not room here to fully explore the 'tension' between Bataille's writings and psychoanalysis. Suffice it to say that Lacan's anal rewriting of Freud is no better equipped to deal with the possibility of psychoanalysis falling away where it is most supposed to matter. This liminal state of psychoanalysis is what makes Kristeva's *Powers of Horror* a more relevant take on the questions raised by Bataille.

8. The original translator commits a serious error in inserting 'climax' for 'entra en jouissance'. Jouissance is not orgasm, even if it can be translated as such. The equivalent to this is in *Eroticism*, where transcendence often slips in instead of excess, exceeding, surpassing. Such versions are notable in that they say what would be precisely the term Bataille is attempting to avoid.

9. One element that is hard to bring out in this context is the deadly and deadpan humour of the text. I shall cite just two examples here to 'give a flavour'. After an ecstatic nude bike-riding incident, Simone is unwell for a time, and she and the narrator play games with eggs in the toilet bowl. At one point, she is sucking his eye, and 'she pisse[s] noisily on the bobbing eggs with total vigour and satisfaction.

At this point she could be regarded as cured' (34; 38 trans. mod.). Later on, Simone has just strangled the priest while fucking him, and as the come trickles down her legs, the narrator feels paralysed 'by my love for the girl and the death of the unspeakable [innommable] creature. I have never been so happy' (65; 67 trans. mod.).

10. For a detailed reconstruction of masochism that challenges Freud's reductionist 'sado-masochism', see Deleuze, *Coldness and Cruelty*, 9–138.

11. Bataille uses the term *homme*, rather than *personne* or *individu*, as he does on many occasions, providing further material for the argument that this tussle with subjectivity is really a male concern.

12. Louis Ferdinand Céline is a novelist notorious both for his experimental writing and his misanthropy, which is often specifically anti-Semitic. For Kristeva the abject individual, particularly in terms of writers, is invariably male. Many writers would in fact take women to have at least as much 'access' to abjection – for example thorough eating disorders. For useful developments of the notion of abjection, see Elizabeth Grosz, *Volatile Bodies* and Judith Butler, *Gender Trouble*, even if both texts downplay the paradoxical nature of abjection. Butler arguably modifies and echoes what in a way was Bataille's point about the exclusion of the 'lower' classes, in arguing that homosexuality becomes a site of abjection for heterosexual society, in *Bodies That Matter*.

7

Art and Aesthetics

Even before Bataille formulates the thought of the general economy, his writings on art point the way towards it, rejecting the modern period's separation of culture into distinct spheres (Lessing, Kant). Instead, he seeks to bring art into contact with sacrifice, eroticism, violence and with questions of the origin and functioning of societies. Art occupies a clear place in the *œuvre* of Bataille as part of the movement of that which is 'beyond' but not transcendent. Excessive would not be transcendent because that would imply it was conveying some true spiritual value. Much art fails to be excessive, content to depict, rather than 'communicate', is Bataille's general argument, but art can be part of sovereignty, general economy. This echoes what he writes about poetry, which often features as part of a list of things that exceed the everyday, 'restricted' economy, while also being often worthy only of contempt. The text that we encounter today as readers, however, sites art, in Bataille, as part of the troubled boundary that defines our existence and the inevitable possibility of our death.

Bataille would reject the term 'aesthetics' as it already concedes the defeat of art, its restriction to a certain realm, which entails its placement as part of an economy of utility, within which the end and means are clear. This does not prevent him effectively from 'doing' aesthetics, at certain points, but we should be wary of defining a Bataillean aesthetics. At another level there could feasibly be a very obvious 'Bataillean aesthetics' – one which would valorize art that aspired to destruction. This can operate at two levels, one formal, the other to do with content. Bataille only favours art that is in some way the destruction of art, *such that the working and place of art can be revealed*, but often this takes a very literal or figurative form: Bataille is very literal-minded in this, and does have much more of an interest in art that depicts scenes of violence, anguish and so on.[1] Krauss and Bois have signalled, in *Formless: A User's Guide*, that along with this focus on content, Bataille seems wilfully ignorant of key developments in modern art, and misses out on areas where formal experimentation would feasibly link up more fruitfully with his thought.

Various questions arise when looking at Bataille's take on art (I am specifically addressing the visual arts here), some of which are Bataille's questions, and others of which are brought to us through the text, despite Bataille's particular, explicit emphases. Firstly, what is the place of art – this is perhaps the big question of the pre-war texts; secondly, what kind of subjectivity do we see in the figure of the artist; thirdly, and this is where we need to extrapolate, what is the role, function or position of representation and figuration in the light of the general economy?

The Place of Art

For us today, the most obvious place for art is the museum. Reproducibility of the work of art, in the form of images in books

through the halls of culture maintains an attitude of reverence, even a 'profound communion' (23; 240) with the objects, but these objects, at least in this setting, are not worthy, do not represent something communal, in Bataille's sense, as 'the paintings are only dead surfaces' (22; 239). It is the coming together as a crowd that interests Bataille. In short, museums provide a cleansing function, ensuring that the desire to exceed mundanity is constrained to the Sunday visit to the museum (the development of 'leisure' fulfils a similar function), and the art itself can lose any danger it may have held. In a sense prior to all this, however, is Bataille's claim that the display of culture hides the spectacle of death that allowed culture to come to the people. The modern museum as we know it 'would thus be linked to the development of the guillotine' (22; 239).

For Bataille, Western architecture (including its antecedents) has always sought to cover up death. Our view of the birth of humanity centres not just on a philosophical recognition of death as defining humanity, but also on the built commemorations that we find even among the Neanderthals. As Hollier notes, in *Against Architecture*, Bataille writes against this architecture and the architecture of thought that accompanies it. Architecture, especially in the form of the monumental (official) building, imposes itself as power. It is more than simply a reflection of power.

> the ideal being of society, that which orders and prohibits with authority, expresses itself in what are architectural compositions in the strict sense of the term. Thus, the great monuments are raised up like dams, pitting the logic of majesty and authority against all the shady elements: it is in the form of cathedrals and palaces that Church and State speak and impose silence on the multitudes. (Bataille, 'Architecture', 21; *OC* I, 171)

Bataille is reflexive as to his own position on the status of architecture. As 'the human order is bound up from the start with the architectural order' (21; 172), you cannot attack one without attacking the other. In this early article we see the firm rejection of humanism as something tied up with authority, imbued with use value and the refusal of excess.

Lest we think that the heroic artist combats this, Bataille notes that 'the great compositions of certain painters express the will to restrict the spirit to an official ideal' (21; 171). This is not because there is a dominant ideology that filters down from the State, but because all areas of society partake of order in its own right. He is not referring to art and patronage or 'official art', but to certain forms of art, as 'the disappearance of academic construction in painting, on the other hand, leaves the way open for expression (even going as far as exaltation) of psychological processes that are most incompatible with social stability' (ibid.). Modern art can be a way of going 'against architecture'.

Art and the Sacred

Modern art does not, for Bataille, do something that is totally new. It partakes of something that all societies, except early modern and modern Western society, have known: the importance of excess, sacrifice, eroticism and death. So modern art is the restoration of a lost continuity. This continuity is not a return, as something has altered: we no longer believe in the existence of fixed truths.

> It appears after the fact that art, no longer capable of expressing whatever it is that, coming to it from outside, is incontestably *sacred* – romanticism having used up the possibilities of renewal – it appears after the fact that art could no longer live if it did not have the force to attain the *sacred instant* by its own resources. The techniques put into play up to that point only had to express a *given* that had its own value and meaning. ('The Sacred', 241; *OC* I, 561)

Art of the early modern period (prior to mid-nineteenth-century

divine power which belongs to him. Nor can he know if this heritage will *consume* and *destroy* the one it *consecrates*. ('The Sacred', 245; *OC* I, 563)

So Bataille sees the period when modern art comes into being as a time of *access*, when what he would later call the 'sovereign artist' is in the same position as the sacrificer in societies with a conception of the violence of the sacred. But the beyond to which this artist accedes is just a beyond – there is no content there.

In his early writings in particular, we see Bataille emphasizing the personal aspect of the artist, in an attempt to delineate possible sacrificial paths for sovereignty. Van Gogh provides the paradigm for the artist as sacrificer, and Bataille is just as fascinated by Van Gogh's cutting off his ear as by the paintings. For Bataille, the two are not simply phenomena we could ascribe to Van Gogh's individual madness. Rather, Van Gogh has found what the Aztec priests had with regard to the sun: there is something beyond the self that the self can lose itself in ('Sacrificial Mutilation and the Severed Ear of Van Gogh', *OC* I, 262). The cutting of the ear released the sun to come *through* Van Gogh ('Van Gogh Prométhée', *OC* I, 499). It is not that this artist has acquired something – rather he has lost the restraints that made him a unified subject, through the 'expenditure' that threatens stable existence (*OC* I, 498), and has moved into a realm of 'inner experience' ('Sacrificial Mutilation and the Severed Ear of Van Gogh', 67; *OC* I, 264).

The artist is called on by Bataille to be more than just an artist (who in accepting such a role accepts the dominance of use value), but where artists are not supposed to go is down the path of commitment (*engagement*), as he continually states in his postwar articles (see *OC* XI, particularly the many articles on Camus, and references to Sartre), because commitment should not be *to* something, but just be there in a 'pure' form.[2]

Surrealism

Much is made of Bataille's link to surrealism, on the basis of his personal engagement with the surrealist movement and his battles with Breton. Like Bataille, surrealism seeks to escape the confines of thought and art of its time, and Bataille has a strong sympathy with parts of its programme, but it seems to me that he always regards surrealism as a failure, and that he is writing 'against surrealism' in much the same way as he writes against architecture.[3] The problem with surrealism is that in trying to get 'above' (*sur*) it elevates the low (the erotic, the violent, the deadly) and thereby makes it into a *value* and

> the resulting adulterations matter little to the surrealists: that the unconscious is no more than a pitiable treasure-trove; that Sade, emasculated by his cowardly apologists, takes on the form of a moralising idealist. . . . All claims from below have been scurrilously disguised as claims from above: and the surrealists, having become the laughingstock of those who have seen close up a sorry and shabby failure, obstinately hold on to their magnificent Icarian pose. ('The "Old Mole" and the Prefix *Sur*', 39; *OC* II, 103)

Surrealism, then, becomes little more than therapy – for society, for the artist. What is interesting is that Bataille does not regard failure as definitive – at least surrealism has tried. His tone after the war is much more conciliatory to both Breton and surrealism in general, but all that has altered is that the general economy leads Bataille to view Icarian failure as one of the possible 'heights' of sovereignty.

The problem that surrealism never eludes is that of being an aesthetic movement, despite its conversion to communism and extolling of psychoanalysis (partially shared by Bataille, at least insofar as he shares surrealism's aims). If surrealism had tried this a bit more convincingly, it would have met Bataille's criteria for

('L'esprit moderne et le jeu des transpositions', 273). The fetishist is exceeded by the erotic connection with the object; the art lover maintains a safe distance. In more general terms the consumption of art can be more sacrificial, refusing to accept the boundaries of taste, criteria of skill on the part of the painter, art knowledge on the part of the viewer.

In an article on a painting by Dalí, Bataille writes that Dalí makes him want 'to squeal like a pig before his canvases' ('The Lugubrious Game', 28; *OC* I, 215). Along the way Dalí and Picasso are seen to 'differ from each other as much as a cloud of flies from an elephant' (30n.; 213n.). The former was less than taken with Bataille's article, and refused to let him use a copy of the picture, but Bataille is, in his own way, praising Dalí, emphasizing that he had shown us the low, dirty side of the unconscious.[4] If art can still inspire us, 'after the death of God', then for Bataille, it has to force out of us a reaction that exceeds rationality.

Myth

Before the war, Bataille sees hope in the form of 'myth', as myth is what is present in genuine communities – they embody myth and myth embodies them. Above all, myth inspires the kind of community that exists only in the festival, in sacrifice. For the individual, '*myth* remains at the disposal of one who cannot be satisfied by art, science or politics' ('The Sorcerer's Apprentice', 232; *OC* I, 535), and in the exceeding of the individual,

> myth alone returns, to the one who is broken by every ordeal, the image of a plenitude extended to the community where men gather. Myth alone enters the bodies of those it binds and it expects from them the same receptiveness. It is the frenzy of every dance; it takes existence 'to its boiling point': it communicates to it the tragic emotion that makes its sacred intimacy possible. (ibid.)

Myth is given no content by Bataille, but the implication is that there will be myths, in the form of stories, even if the 'height' of existence lies in the moment they fall away. This falling away is all that separates him from the Fascist vision of uniting 'the people' through myth and action.

After the war, myth is presented somewhat differently. Now Bataille speaks of the 'absence of myth'. Instead of myth filling, however ironically, the space vacated by God (perhaps, for the artist, in the form of a 'personal symbolism'), myth now signals its failure – there is no myth left, our last story is this absence. Awareness of this is no less a belief than that granted any other myth and is the further revelation that even emptiness is only belief, belief only emptiness: 'the absence of myth is also a myth: the coldest, the purest, the only *true* myth' ('The Absence of Myth', 48; *OC* XI, 236). Surrealism is one of the movements that has never made this leap, content to play around with aesthetics, believing that somewhere a truth lurked. At another level, surrealism is part of the absence of myth in the sense that it *is* a myth without foundation, and therefore responds to the mythlessness of capitalist modernist, restricted society. However, it cannot be an answer, because there is no answer, and although it is not explicit, maybe the fact of this 'absence of myth' being our only myth, *and therefore our only truth*, is Bataille's equivalent to Adorno's question about the possibility of poetry 'after Auschwitz'.[5]

This 'fundamental' lack or emptiness should be taken as underpinning Bataille's longer writings on art that he produced in the 1950s and was working on up to his death. Much of this work is taken up with questions of 'the origin of art', and origins, for Bataille, are only ever retrospective, even if at first sight his stream of assertions seem to add up to a belief in a true origin. Only our lack of myth/truth enables us to look back, for example, at the cave paintings in the way Bataille wishes to, as this is the period before

many others, and in particular the artists of the time, he had already emphasized the link between 'primitive' art and modern(ist) art.[6]

In *Lascaux*, Bataille presents and analyses the array of pictures that had been unearthed, and brings them into his 'system'. Here was proof of what he had been arguing, and here was not just what had been present 'at the beginning' but more importantly, what was untainted by the accretions of truths, and could now be looked at through a modern 'absence of myth'. *Lascaux* and the later *Tears of Eros* try to set out the centrality of art, along with death, eroticism and so on. They are not always convincing, and Bataille is often drawn into just marvelling at the violence and raw beauty of the cave paintings. Whilst this is in some ways an updating of his suggestions about experiencing art intimately, it is annoying in the long run.

Lascaux brings an addition to the 'system' of general economy. Previously, death is the 'différantial' term, both bringing humanity, and being what lies beyond humanity. Eroticism fills exactly the same position, and so, as a result of these two, does 'discontinuous being' – our existence as discrete individuals. In addition, awareness of death brings the possibility or, perhaps, the requirement not to squander but to accumulate, to preserve. This in turn breeds the 'accursed share' where expenditure becomes the outside that was 'always already' outside. Into this paradoxical beginning of humanity (always to be glimpsed in retrospect) comes art. In looking at the 'origin of humanity', we have looked to evidence of the commemoration of the dead, and also the existence of tools. Bataille adds that the introduction of art and of play are also significant (*Lascaux*, 27; *OC* IX, 28), and goes on to say that awareness of death and the world of work and accumulation (which includes language) is not all that are required to be human. Whilst it would hardly be new to say that humanity exists due to its capacity to create, what might be of more interest is the fact that, for Bataille, this capacity is absolutely bound up with death, eroticism and the rejection (through utility) of what is most creative. He writes that 'art, play and transgression only come about together, in a unique movement of the negation of the principles which preside over the regularity of work' (*Lascaux*, 38; *OC*

IX, 41). This coming together happens under the auspices of transgression and taboo which, as in *Eroticism*, constitutes another version of 'the' origin. As a result, all art should aim to transgress (*Lascaux*, 39; *OC* IX, 42).

So what we have here is more (or less) than a dialectic. Negation, or something like *différance*, is at work/play; death as negation forms awareness of life; this in turn informs work; art, then, is the next negation. Except that having become this negation, art is transgression of the limits of work. Death, too, has become transgression. The taboo, even in the form of work, is only the going against what was before it, and *this is only informed by what comes after*. Once death, art, eroticism or whatever becomes the outside, the other, it is then also at the beginning: instead of a progress of negations, there is only an endless crossing and re-crossing of lines. In this, art is perfect, as it is both work and the excess of work ('Dossier de Lascaux', *OC* IX, 341).

Another paradox awaits us, in the largely straightforward description of the violent and erotic scenes of the cave paintings. This paradox is to do with something like 'the birth of figuration'. According to Bataille, the painters of Lascaux show us their humanness in figuring animality – or at least what we might consider, once 'inside humanity', as animal (*Lascaux*, 115; *OC* IX, 62). This animality is on its way out, and what we see in the pictures is both this loss, and that this loss is what defines humanity (mourning might be too strong a term, however). The human heads are disfigured, or are replaced by animal heads (see also 'l'art primitif', *OC* I, 251). 'In the sacred moment of figuration, they seem to

frightening for a long time' (123; *OC* IX, 72). I note this comment largely because it is so representative of his throwaway references to women and is not essential to his thought at all, but is potentially damaging, due to its arbitrariness.

The Tears of Eros adds little to the points made in *Lascaux*. It tries to establish the lineage between the erotic, death-oriented art of the caves and Western art insofar as it has pursued transgression, sex, death. The collection of images and accompanying text come across as overly thematic, presuming an untroubled link between excess and its representation, which contradicts most, if not all, of Bataille's theories. Essentially, the book relies on the presumption that a violent enough scene, conveyed with some violence, can stimulate the 'inner experience' of community through sacrifice or violence. 'This book, for its author [writes Bataille of *The Tears of Eros*], has only one meaning: *it opens up consciousness of the self*' (*The Tears of Eros*, 142; *OC* X, 620). Now, maybe this is only meant to apply to him, in the process of writing, but it is clearly an attempt to reach at least some of its readers through an 'absent community'. Perhaps the most interesting part is the revelation of the 'Chinese torture' pictures that he had been mentioning over the years. The pictures show scenes, at the beginning of the century, of a young Chinese man being dismembered, and wearing a look of ecstasy. Bataille had an ecstatic reaction to the picture, and this had led him on to think of the merging of religious and erotic ecstasies through violence (206; 627). The book closes with what could be seen as the completion of the story opened in Lascaux:

> Religion in its entirety was founded upon sacrifice. But only an interminable detour allows us to reach that instant where the contraries seem visibly conjoined, where the religious horror disclosed in sacrifice becomes linked to the abyss of eroticism, to the last shuddering tears that eroticism alone can illuminate. (207; 627)

There are various problems here. In his desire to affirm, Bataille has given too much of an answer – we seem to have finally emerged from the light, blinking into the dark, and the dark is true. Images seem to serve as means to another end, and are therefore caught within a restricted economy. Further to this point is that Bataille has become overly obsessed with content, and has neglected to notice that the pictures, however alarming they might be in their clarity, allow us some control. It would be more interesting at least to include more firmly the aspect of formal 'horror' or 'ecstasy'.

On the more positive side, the book offers a possible way out of the impasse of having to organize thought to disorganize it, of having to offer discourse where its destruction was what was wanted. *The Tears of Eros* stands as a version of Bataille's system put in play, where the strength of the discourse cannot help. The images allow a silence to speak, one which Bataille thinks sufficient enough to provoke a reaction, through contagion. The book is highly personalized, which some might regard as a good thing, but even this element is only of worth if taken in the light of his writings on sovereignty, eroticism and the general economy; otherwise it is a slightly painful (as in poor) avowal of his own subjectivity.

Form

Bataille does not neglect the issue of form in art (he is very reticent to think about form in literature). His work on Manet is a good example of this concern, and a much more successful merging of his obsessions and theories than the attempt made in *Tears of Eros*. In *Manet*, Bataille makes the now familiar claim that Manet should be seen as the start of the modern movement, at least within art, both because of his subject matter, and because of his treatment of it.[7]

Unlike purely abstract art, Manet's takes a subject and empties it. The subject is maintained as an absence that echoes (and even comes before) the death of God. Indifference is part of this process, and Bataille cites Manet's reworking of Goya's picture of the assassination of Emperor Maximilian (52–5; 133–4). This indifference is a revolt against the vacuous persistence of old forms of art, and he moves toward sovereignty through 'the silence of art' (58; 135) and the *silencing* of art. *Olympia*'s prostitute is all of this, the bearer of an aggressive indifference, manifesting a low eroticism, and with Manet disdainful in the 'underpainted' detail, her 'presence has the simplicity of an absence' (67; 142), bringing sovereignty not to what is figured, but to the process of (de) figuration.

Olympia is about the loss of narrative, a narrative that does get started, only to be lost, as 'what this picture signifies is not text but [text] being wiped away' (67; 142). Above all, *Olympia* is an attack on *all* that is solid: '*Olympia*, like modern poetry, is the negation of this world: the negation of Olympus, of the poem, of the mythological monument, of the monument and of monumental conventions' (71; 145). This reading stands as a potentially crucial moment in the Bataillean *œuvre*, indicating how nihilism is there, how NOTHING 'is', when (dis)appearing through a figured image: in other words, 'pure' destruction is of no interest, compared to the slow burning emptiness that signals the impossibility of the nothing lurking inside (when it is supposed to be outside, far away).

The subject of the painting – the person being painted, in their subjectivity – is also subject to attack. Manet's way of painting an individual, his way of emptying the subjectivity and draining the surroundings, 'is like sacrifice, *is* sacrifice', one 'which alters, which destroys, which kills the victim, *without neglecting it*' (103; 157). As a result, Manet's painting is not so much interesting for what is in it as for what it does (102; 156).

Formless

To conclude this survey of Bataille's 'aesthetic', we return to an early piece, 'Formless' (*Visions of Excess*, 31; 'Informe', *OC* I, 217), as this has stimulated one of the essential recent works on modern and contemporary art: Krauss and Bois's *Formless: A User's Guide.* Rather than repeat what they have done (which is to formulate a Bataillean aesthetics of modern art, and apply it), I will draw attention to some points arising from their text, in terms of Bataille's thought in general. Krauss and Bois take 'formless' and make of it a way of theorizing process (amongst other things), arguing on the basis that, according to Bataille, 'a dictionary begins when it no longer gives the meaning of words, but their tasks' (Bataille, 'Formless', 31; *OC* I, 217), and that 'formless' is the beginning of this new dictionary.[9] 'Formless' is also what lies outside the dictionary, that which is covered up in the assigning of forms, and it therefore operates as the *différance* between Form and Formlessness.

Krauss and Bois do not take the next step, which is to note that 'formless' too is a form, a way of encapsulating 'that which escapes form', so is trapped within the world of form, rather than being a resistance to it, or its inherent unravelling. Insofar as it is an unravelling, it is that which is within the giving of forms, and cannot *be*. If we look at the last sentence of 'Formless', we can see that Bataille signals formless as the arbitrariness, the impossibility, the non-event of form that form hides (like presence to absence, life to death and so on): 'affirming that the universe resembles nothing and is only *formless* amounts to saying that the universe is something like a spider or a gob of spit' (31; 217 trans. mod.). As with chaos mathematics, it is a mistake to think that 'formless' is the site or process of the loss of forms – rather it is a new way of looking at how form coalesces – a way that entails thinking the continual movement between something and nothing, form and lack of form.

some kind of sublime where the process of representation is exceeded. In this excess, the individual loses their isolated subjectivity and joins with the loss 'presented' by a work of art. Even if Bataille never really moves far from such an idea, excess is written in a way that is the opposite of the sublime as some kind of regulating device, some way of letting off ontological steam. Throughout his writings, loss, waste, death, sacrifice and so on are determining, in the end, and not adjuncts. His writings on art contain both the best and the worst elements of his obsessions: on the one hand we get dynamic dispersal of form, content, subjectivity; on the other, a simplistic liking for a pseudo-gothic aesthetic.

Notes

1. He does not entirely neglect the formal side, especially before the war. In a short article on Miró, for example, he praises the painter for pursuing the destruction of painting, for enacting its 'de-composition' ('*décomposition*') ('Joan Miró: peintures récentes', *OC* I, 255). He also writes that modern art is sacrificial in form ('L'art, exercice de cruauté' [Art as Practice of Cruelty'], *OC* XI, 482.

2. He cites Picasso as being capable of political painting without subjugating himself to the use value of a movement or particular external aim ('Les peintures politiques de Picasso', *OC* XI, 24–7. *Guernica* is characterized as a site where excess is freed : 25).

3. In one late essay, he reviews his position on surrealism, observing that he has always been against surrealism, but now realizes that he has actually been fighting from within ('A propos d'assoupissements' ['On Torpor'], *OC* XI, 31). While Bataille does soften his line after the war, both toward Breton and to surrealism in general, nothing has actually changed in how he sees surrealism. It is his line on failure that has changed (see Chapter 4 above).

4. Bataille is also very taken with Buñuel and Dalí's *Un Chien andalou* (see 'Eye'). The famous scene where the eye is cut signals death and also the death of reason, as identified by Foucault with regard to the upturned eye in *The Story of the Eye*.

5. See Adorno, *Negative Dialectics*, 361–408. The absence of myth is also essentially tied to the absence of community. Such an absence signals not that we have lost the possibility of community, but that our community must be one of absence, where we lose our selves, rather than restoring a 'true' community with foundations, a project, a clear boundary (see 'Take it or Leave it', 96; *OC* XI, 130–1).

6. See, for example, 'L'art primitif', *OC* I, 247–54. Also, the periodical *Documents*, with which Bataille and many well known artists were involved, had continually and expressly juxtaposed surrealism and other modern forms of art with images and writings on 'primitive' art.

7. *Manet* dates from 1955, and Clement Greenberg was already well on the way to establishing the paradigms of modernity and modernism as they appear in art criticism (in 'Avant-Garde and Kitsch', *Art and Culture*, 3–21 (this essay originally appearing in 1939). Bataille's book coincides with Greenberg's views becoming paradigmatic, as the 1950s are arguably the time when Greenberg's ideas started to become influential (if not in France).

8. The translation of this book is probably the most consistently poor of all, and without the seedy fun of *My Mother/Madame Edwarda/The Dead Man*'s awfulness. I give page references for the existing translation, but all translations are my own.

9. 'Besogne' in the original, which implies not just a task, but an onerous task, a duty. This also militates against the use of 'formless' as 'task', or process being something positive, something which could elude constraints. As with taboo, without constraint, there is no transgression.

8

Politics

From the earliest writings, Bataille's texts are driven by antipathy to modern, Western, capitalist society. If anything, politics is where Bataille is at his most consistent, even if, as usual, there are shifts in emphasis and counter-intuitive moves on his part. When we look to assess his political position(s), we have to cover two distinct aspects: his stated positions, whether to do with the political position of others, his own, or his view on politics as a category of activity; and the political implications of his writings. The first set of aspects is the one that I will deal with directly here, and from these I will draw out some of the political implications.

The principal period in which Bataille is most like the figure of the *engagé*, or committed, writer is the late 1930s. In the articles of this time, he moves from an emphasis on the valorization of practices from outside modern society to a more overt criticism of capitalism as an essential part of the problem that is modern society. The obvious inference is that the rise of Fascism drove this interest. Similarly, not only was the Soviet Union's alternative significant at the time in its own right, it too was heading in a very similar direction to Fascism, and taking on a new significance.

During and after the war, Bataille becomes much more of a commentator on politics as such, as an area of human existence, arguing against the apparent need for praxis to be realized in the figure of the committed writer, who should advocate action.

Politics, for Bataille himself, suffers the same fate as economics within the general economy: with perfect consistency, politics cannot be seen as an autonomous realm, except in the reductionism of restricted economies. With *The Accursed Share*, Bataille shifts to rethinking what others call politics as movement within general economy and across to restricted economy. Everything is either accumulation and utility or waste and sacrifice. Despite, or perhaps because of this, he advocates the continued existence of Stalinism – not because it is the only hope, but because it performs a specific function, even in its cruelty, in diminishing the bourgeois, capitalist, Christian individual he considers essentially limited. Late texts such as *Eroticism* might suggest a politics of sexual liberation, and later essays firmly suggest revolt, refusal, as a means of subversion. Above all, there is a strong sense of continuity in Bataille's views on politics, but in looking at this continuity we should not lose sight of the paradoxes or difficulties in these positions. This chapter focuses on essays from throughout his *œuvre*, and largely leaves the political implications of the major works to the discussions in earlier chapters.

Capitalism and Marxism

Capitalist, or bourgeois, society (Bataille tends to blur the cultural and economic) is a reduction of man's potential in an existence of homogeneity. '*Homogeneous* society is productive society, namely _____ Structure of Fascism', 138; *OC*

of an individual – the possibility of sovereign existence away from calculations of utility (this is Bataille's line from the mid-1930s in essays such as 'The Psychological Structure of Fascism' right through to the texts explicitly on sovereignty in the late 1950s, including *The Accursed Share,* vol. *III: Sovereignty)*. Capitalism removes the artisanal link to the thing made, and makes us all producers, means instead of ends, making means instead of being ends. Bataille's story is very similar to that told by Marx, but we can see in Bataille's texts so many elements of discord with Marx that we might wonder what is left of the latter in the former (who whilst not avowing himself a communist, due to his distrust of political parties, certainly saw himself as being more or less of a Marxist).

He writes that Marxism is right about the 'infrastructure' of modern society ('The Psychological Structure of Fascism', 137; *OC* I, 339), but that it neglects the relevance 'of the modalities peculiar to the formation of religious and political society' (137; 339). Marxists would of course argue that they have thought about these aspects, and that all the effects are at least linked, if not determined, by the economic base. It is notable that by 'infrastructure' here Bataille means 'base structure', but his term should be read as an indication of the distance of Bataille's text (and in the wider sense, his *œuvre)*, within which economics is not a means to other ends, from Marxism.[1]

Bataille argues that religion is significant in that, in the form of Christianity, it works with capitalist society to dispose of the sacred. What distinguishes this from Marx and Marxism is that for them, there is nothing beyond the material. An even earlier essay notes this problem, in a way that is only implicit in the essays of the period after 1933:

> Most materialists, even though they may have wanted to do away with all spiritual entities, ended up positing an order of things whose hierarchical relations mark it as specifically idealist. They situated dead matter at the summit of a conventional hierarchy of diverse facts, without perceiving that in this way they gave in to an obsession with the *ideal* form of matter. ('Materialism', 15; *OC* I, 179)

So materialism cannot be the only answer, and in the light of these comments, which are perfectly consistent with all the political writings of the 1930s and the postwar texts, we can make the case that Marxism is no more than a version of restricted economy. The sacred would be that which exceeds such a concept, and is communal in that it is the loss of self in a greater whole (even if this whole is nothing).

Religion 'is the source of social authority' ('The Psychological Structure of Fascism', 152; *OC* I, 360), on the basis that its authority does not come from personal value, as is the case with military authority. Neither does the authority that comes with religion just represent one form of misleading 'the people' in order to attain power. Religion is a particular process within the development of society: 'the supreme being of theologians and philosophers represents the most profound introjection of the structure characteristic of *homogeneity* into *heterogeneous* existence' (153; 361). So the invention of God both reduces the sacred and makes God sovereign in the Bataillean sense, as he is beyond the everyday. His place then gets taken by the Idea, the ideal. The arrival of gods, particularly a single god, provides the ground for the creation of temporal power, and indicates that the question of general economy precedes that of economics as a version of the master/slave dialectic (remembering that Bataille's own 'version' of the dialectic also undoes dialectical logic).

The creation of social authority leads us into the realm of political authority, a further homogenization. From here, Bataille goes direct to the State, missing out the Marxist link to an economic base. But once we arrive in the State, modern society *is* structured in a way that economic, and creates new forms of poverty and of power, ecoa liberal State, none of which, Bataille notes, has ever been altered through revolution into a communist society ('Vers la révolution réelle' ['Towards Real Revolution'], *OC* I, 417).[2]

But Bataille is far from rejecting the possibility of revolution, or the revolutionary potential of the working class. In a way that is perhaps closer to anarchism, he emphasizes the need for, or even the inevitability of, the rising of the wretched in general – and there is no reason why this could not later include the bourgeois themselves. It is not economic necessity alone that will drive the revolution. It will come as the result of the 'anguish provoked among the working classes by the birth of the three all-powerful States' ('Le problème de l'État', 336) (these being Germany, Italy and the Soviet Union). Fascism has come from the problems of liberal societies (it is *not*, for Bataille, simply an outgrowth of the capitalist system), but needs to be fought by 'organic movements', and not via dated communist conceptions of the Party leading the industrial working class, leading everyone else ('Vers la révolution réelle', 420). 'Organic movements' come about at specific times, in response to events (422), and are able to attack the multiple targets presented by 'democratic' or Fascist society. We might, however, wonder whether this organic movement is not too close to Fascism.

Fascism

There might be more than a suggestion that Bataille has gone too far, and, given the climate of the 1930s, is heading towards Fascism. Above all what we see in the often implicit rejection of central elements of Marxism is an attempt to deal with why Fascism was happening, and this attempt does lead to moments of ambiguity. This does not prevent Bataille from continually stating his opposition to Fascism and nationalism ('The Psychological Structure of Fascism'; the articles defending Nietzsche; the 'Contre-attaque' [Counter-attack] movement),[3] but the ambiguity is present especially when he writes on 'heterogeneity'.

According to Bataille, the heterogeneous realm is all that is outside norms, the controls of modern society. Fascism exceeds and challenges liberal society, and is heterogeneous because it aims *above* and *beyond* the utilitarian concerns of capitalism. It appeals to what is 'noble' ('The Psychological Structure of Fascism', 145; *OC* I, 350), and its cruelty and purity elevate it above homogeneity (146; 351). Fascism exceeds class boundaries, creating an organic social movement (154; 363). Thus far, it might be construed that maybe Fascism does have something to offer, and although he does not state it as such, for Bataille it does match some aspiration neglected by utilitarian society. However, as well as the overt renunciations of Fascism, he has specific theoretical points to make which disqualify it. Firstly, Fascism's use of the nation as organizing concept reintroduces homogeneity (154–5; 363–4), and this homogeneity is solidified in the concentration of power that is the totalitarian State. In a later article, he writes that Nazism is nowhere near as grand as it thinks it is. Whilst it could have been an 'epic' force, it is nothing more than a simplistic, militaristic form of nationalism ('Nietzsche est-il fasciste?' ['Is Nietzsche a Fascist?'], *OC* XI, 9). This authoritarianism renders Fascism 'a servile discipline' ('Contre-attaque: Appel à l'action' ['Counter-attack: Call to Action'], *OC* I, 396).

Bataille's attack on Fascism is closely tied to his defence of Nietzsche's writings, which he argues are incompatible with Nazism. He writes that Nietzsche's writing is way beyond Nazism, and that 'the distance between Hitler and Nietzsche is that of a police room compared to the heights of the Alps' ('Nietzsche est-il fasciste?', *OC* XI, 11). Furthermore, he is beyond all use – he is simply not reducible: 'NIETZSCHE'S DOCTRINE CANNOT BE ... Fascists', 184; *OC* I, 450).[4]

the general economy? The short answer seems to be there is good and bad expenditure. How then can he be sanguine about the 'becoming object' that Stalinism was still inflicting on its population? He certainly musters what could be seen as a chilling response to Hiroshima, arguing that we only want to believe it exceptional because then we can continue ignoring the fact that millions of deaths will always occur anyway 'Concerning the Accounts Given by the Residents of Hiroshima, 221–35; *OC* XI, 172–87). I am not at all rejecting his position on the Holocaust, rather observing that it seems significant that he is unable to place it anywhere in his various systems (unlike Hiroshima). This might be to do with the enormity of the event, the impossibility of incorporating it. But Bataille has a 'system' that can account for this, so it is particularly interesting that it is further removed from discourse by not being included.

Another statement worth pausing on is about the 'sovereign sacrifice' that Hitler makes in pursuing the battle of Stalingrad long after it is lost (recalling that a sovereign sacrifice is not heroism, but pointless destruction or loss). One of the reasons Nazism haunts us, remaining our heterogeneous other, is that it is both at the height of reason, with its efficiency, and at the height of monstrosity, again due to its efficiency. Bataille's way of raising this is in the rejection of utilitarianism that is the disaster of Stalingrad ('Caprice et machinerie d'État à Stalingrad' ['Whim and State Machine at Stalingrad'], *OC* XI, 472–9).

The period after the war sees Bataille treating ideologies from a theoretical perspective that differs from his earlier approach. Fascism is now seen only in its results, its destruction and murder. Liberal society is not let off the hook, and communism is rethought – or, more accurately, its relevance is restated, with the peculiar valorization of the Stalinist Soviet Union (see Chapter 4 above). The last decisive shift to note concerns the base of politics: action.

Revolution, Violence, Action

Bataille's notion of political action alters significantly after the war. Before the war, he has a notion of the possibility of positive political action. Conceivably, the simple reason for this is the context of the threat of various nationalist, Fascist and right-wing organizations (France had monarchist as well as nationalist elements in its right wing). The deeper reason is perhaps to do with the stage Bataille had reached in his philosophy: he had gone far enough to wish to see the overthrow of the capitalist system, but not as far as to disbelieve in the possibility of any alternative. He did, for example, believe that surrealism opened up possibilities, but that it was doomed by the fact that logically it could not succeed. Possibly the defining political paradox in Bataille is the necessity to do something, and that this something will fail. Surrealism, however, rejects sovereign failure in favour of aesthetic success and limits.

Bataille's notion of action alters, and before the war, moves gradually toward an anarchist perspective. Whilst he accepts Marx's critique of capitalism, Bataille is suspicious of the methods of communism and its results. This is not just to do with an awareness of the problems of Stalinism, but is also an increasingly critical view of the Popular Front alliance of communists and socialists that effectively ended up defending the capitalist system ('A ceux qui n'ont pas oublie la guerre du droit et de la liberté' ['To those who have not forgotten the just war for freedom'], *OC* I, 399–401). Whilst the defence against Fascism is the essential point of the Popular Front, Bataille and Contre-attaque regarded it as equally important that it attack capitalism, and *attack* Fascism ('Popular Front in the Street', 165; *OC* I, 401). The Popular Front is close to his conception of an 'organic movement', representing an outbreak of discontent, but it needs to keep the 'contagion' of popular movement going. Here we begin to

characterize as Bataille's ultra-leftism:

control. The revolution can only be 'effervescence' ('En attendant la grève générale' ['Waiting for the General Strike'], *OC* II, 254), and this brings in a sacrificial notion of politics. The question is, what exactly is being sacrificed? Capitalism is to be attacked, but the problem is that the revolution, in Bataille's terms, cannot really serve a purpose, as it would then have a use value.

Like Bakunin, Bataille seems to suggest that violence itself can bring about a change, without bringing a particular change: it is the violence that is creative.[6] He writes that we attribute use value to revolution, but destruction is the real core of such action ('The Use Value of D.A.F. de Sade', 100; *OC* II, 67). This mirrors the potlatch, where sacrifice does lead to acquisition of rank, even if the activity is essentially against all ends other than sacrifice. Also, 'it is obvious that all destruction that is neither useful nor inevitable can only be the achievement of an exploiter' (100; 67). Here, the reference is to the destruction of something in particular, as in 'imperial war' (102n.; 67n.), because the essay then goes on to specify the 'purest' form of destruction:

> Without a profound complicity with natural forces such as violent death, gushing blood, sudden catastrophes and the horrible cries of pain that accompany them, terrifying ruptures of what had seemed to be immutable, the fall into stinking filth of what had been elevated – without a sadistic understanding of an incontestably thundering and torrential nature, there could be no revolutionaries, there could only be a revolting utopian sentimentality. (101; 67)

To return to the question of the Holocaust – because it served a purpose, however mindless and dreadful, it does not count as revolutionary action. A more troubling case (with regard to the above logic) could perhaps be seen in the Serbia/Kosovo situation. NATO fought a war at a distance, unwilling to suffer any loss – is this 'revolting utopian sentimentality' compared to Serbia's continual brutality? In practice, NATO's hands are far from clean, but their way of fighting war ('surgical strikes' against Iraq) could conceivably be seen as worse than the cruel abandon of genocide in the course of war. I am not suggesting Bataille believes this to be the case, but the implication of his more Sadean statements is that excessive destruction will happen, come what may, and we have to understand this. The worst, or the least aware, position is the one that replaces war with a process of 'hygiene' – the 'grounds' for many genocides – and, of course, the 'reason' for the gratuitous violence in the former Yugoslavia.

Bataille's position is troubling, and more so when we think of the political implications of what he says when he is not discussing politics as such. Nonetheless, he does believe something new can emerge from violence and sacrifice, but that this cannot be predicted, controlled in advance. For this reason, he is more in the anarchist tradition than the nihilistic one, and more aware of our existence as something communal than Hobbes, Sade or Nietzsche, even if these are his most obvious precursors. Nowhere is there a recommendation that all life should be about destruction – it is to be violent at certain instants, but these moments take their force from being exceptional, and he even writes at one point that the revolution should aim to abolish both violence and property ('[Note sur le système actuel de répression]', '[Note on the Existing System of Repression]' *OC* II, 134).

Bataille's view on politics hardens after the war, in that politics is no longer to be seen as a sphere worthy of intervention. Even in *The Accursed Share*, where he advocates a widening of the Marshall Plan as a form of gift economy, and maintains the need for the existence of the Soviet Union as part of a dialectic of economies, politics is not the site of importance. The general economy subsumes all 'spheres' of modern society. Society is still something that could do with changing, but it seems that it can be left to its own devices, even if more expenditure, in whatever form,

The most obvious target of the critique of committed writing is existentialism, and Sartre in particular. Existentialism must be lived, and not written, or else it is inauthentic, notes Bataille wryly ('De l'existentialisme au primat de l'économie' ['From Existentialism to the Height of Economy'], *OC* XI, 284). As Bataille's own logic implies he should not write, he seems to take great pleasure in existentialism's constant assertion of authenticity just where it cannot take place. Similarly, he writes, with reference to Sartre, that surely the worst of all is to *speak* of action, while not doing it ('Lettre à Merleau-Ponty', *OC* XI, 252).[7] As it is not enough, as a response, or as an alternative, to say that true action is impossible to do or recommend ('Le mensonge politique'['The Lie of Politics'], *OC* XI, 335), perhaps it is the advocacy of action, it is the bringing into discourse of commitment, that is the problem. Politics can still play a role as a 'negative politics' of refusal, of revolt (and Bataille is positive about Camus on this point). This negative politics is still defined through 'the free spirit [. . .] who stays at a distance from judges and torturers' ('Nietzsche – William Blake', *OC* XI, 425), but negative it remains, as 'of all absolute judgements, the most consequential – and the most *debatable* – is the political one. It can no longer be a case of positively taking sides' (ibid.).

So where does this leave us? It is very difficult to see what Bataille offers in terms of politics, at least when he deals explicitly with it. Arguably, his writings provide the basis for many political approaches or strategies, particularly those of new forms of politics, away from the totalizations of traditional political movements. Equally, he might be suggesting 'do nothing', or 'make Fascism better', or 'sacrifice more people'. As with Nietzsche, evidence can be found for many positions and uses, but it is this multiplicity that we should perhaps take from Bataille's texts: there can be no *one* politics. Furthermore, given his critiques of use value, how can we put his writing to use, and be faithful to it? How can we be faithful to it without attributing truth, and therefore an internal utility? We are left with this: Bataille's writings can be used in many ways, including many political ways, but should they be?

Notes

1. In 'The Critique of the Foundations of the Hegelian Dialectic' Bataille argues that the master slave dialectic *as such* has been neglected in the shift to the materialism of Marxism. This is not to say that Marxism should be rejected, as it is 'the living ideology of the modern proletariat' (114; *OC* I, 289–90), just that the economic struggle has only come to seem the most important of many dialectical processes.

2. He often makes this point in the essays of the 1930s. See also 'Contre-attaque: Union de Lutte des Intellectuels Révolutionnaires' ('Contre-attaque: The Fighting Union of Revolutionary Intellectuals', *OC* I, 379–83). The essay cited is effectively a manifesto for the group Contre-attaque, which was an organization of leftists determined to fight both fascism and the liberal state.

3. See, for example, *OC* I, 379–412, where the texts of Contre-attaque are to be found, all of which specify an anti-Fascist position.

4. This impossibility of reduction, of the attribution of clear meaning, should, nonetheless, not be taken as allowing Nietzsche some dubious moments, as, according to Bataille, the one thing we can be certain of is that Nietzsche was vigorously anti-anti-Semitic ('Nietzsche and the Fascists' 182–4; 447–50, for examples).

5. This last article is possibly one of Bataille's most important of the post-war period. In it he comes very close to the approach of the 'phenomenology' of Blanchot, Lévinas and Derrida, in relation to death and the possibility of being, in a way that is not just a reiteration of Heidegger's position. On this last point, it is curious that Heidegger, a member of the Nazi Party, actually produced, in the four-volume *Nietzsche*, the text (along with those of Bataille) that did most to theoretically distance Nietzsche from Nazism, even though Heidegger is far from criticizing Nietzsche in it.

6. Bakunin writes: 'let us trust to the Eternal Spirit which only . . . destroys because it is the inexhaustible and eternally creating source of all life. The urge to destroy is also a creative urge!' ('Reaction in Germany', cited by Aileen Kelly, *Mikhail Bakunin: A Study in the Psychology and Politics of Utopianism*, 94). Bakunin ___ ____ ____ Bataille a sense of the importance of secret societies (see Kelly, *Mikhail ___ _____ __ least, to be heading along the*

End: Silence

Lastly, silence. Throughout his texts, Bataille circles around death, the erotic, laughter, drunkenness, sacrifice, waste, expenditure, dirt, horror – but as well as all of these, there is silence – perhaps the last of the attempts to define the absence, that which is outside of 'me' that structures us as individual subjects. He writes that our humanity consists of a 'middle term', comprising eroticism, sacrifice and so on, and this is the 'nucleus of violent silence' that makes us ('Attraction and Repulsion II', 114; *OC* II, 319). There is silence that spreads from corpses, literally, as we keep silent near them, and 'metaphysically', in that they are silence, our silence (118–19; 326). Silence, like death, is not something simply waiting for us, or that was always there – it is something that is 'always already' there, that arrives as a function of life, of language. Silence is to language what nudity is to clothes – not separate, but absolutely linked. Nudity and silence can only exist after their annulment in clothes or words, and will then be seen as the primordial condition.

Silence is not the final truth – it is the place where truth is undone. *Inner Experience* makes several references to the attempt to attain silence, which in some ways *is* inner experience (29; *OC* V, 41–2). But silence, like sovereignty or death, is not a place that can be inhabited. It is the instant of non-being, or absence of awareness. If this is where your philosophy is leading you, then writing it is a problem, but the writing indicates the absence it cannot be

('Méthode de méditation'; *OC* V, 199). At such points Bataille most resembles Beckett, even to the expression of futility meaning that you cannot even give up 'why continue', he asks, 'but I continue' (*Inner Experience*, 33; *OC* V, 45 trans. mod.).

Bataille does not himself see this link, and although he admires Beckett, he estimates that Beckett only has anything to say about the 'human condition' by accident ('Molloy', *OC*, XII, 86). For Bataille, Beckett is not as profound as Blanchot, who conveys the silence that lies in and around words ('La littérature française en 1952', *OC* XII, 239. Blanchot is dealt with in terms of this writing out of silence in 'Silence et littérature', *OC* XII, 173–8). Bataille feels a great deal of affinity with Blanchot's writings, but seems not to have really paid attention to Beckett, whose writings, in addition to suggesting some form of ontological silence, are full of the ridiculous, the low, the dirty – all much vaunted by Bataille elsewhere.

Writing can take us to silence: Sade's violence is seen as a way of silencing language, discourse (*OC* X, 706n.), as violence prevents discourse, is the stopping of discourse, is difficult to process as discourse. But this violent silence relies on the writing that it tries to stop. Baudelaire is seen as achieving 'a perfect silence of the will' (*Literature and Evil*, 59; *OC* IX, 209), giving himself over to sovereign poetry where meaning is at risk. Manet, in his art, manages to bring into play 'the silence of art' (*Manet*, 58; *OC* IX, 135), through the progressive removal of content and narrative. Violence in the real world takes us out of language, but it is not certain that

silence reinforced by the verbiage of discourse in which silence *is not*.

Eroticism is the site *par excellence* of the 'violent silence', and is the moment of communication where we are 'literally' beyond ourselves (264; 257–8) and silence, death and eroticism are 'against philosophy' (276; 270). Philosophy is exceeded in the writing of silence; individual, discontinuous being is replaced by an emptied nothing: the nothing of Bataille is not an ultimate something, the one thing which is – it is that which is not. The community which is absence of community 'fills up the depths like a wind that empties them' ('Take It or Leave It', 96; *OC* XI, 131 trans. mod.). Talking of silence – it could be death, eroticism, sacrifice – Bataille offers us nothing, a potlatch, an excessive gift that challenges us to pay it back:

> I have been trying to talk a language that equals zero, a language that equals nothing at all, a language which returns to silence. I am not talking about nothingness, which sometimes looks to me like a pretext for adding a specialised chapter onto speech; I am talking about the suppression of whatever language may add to the world. I realise that this suppression cannot be rigorously applied. Anyway the point is not to bring in another sort of duty. But I owe it to myself to put you on guard against an unfortunate use of what I have said. From this point anything that does not take us out of the world [. . .] would betray my purpose. (*Eroticism*, 264; *OC* X, 258)

Bibliography

Bataille's texts in English are listed in alphabetical order, along with their location in the *Œuvres complètes* (*OC*). The French texts referred to in this book are listed in the order in which they occur in *OC*. The order in which texts appear in *OC* approximates the order in which they were written.

Bataille: in English

L'Abbé C (London: Marion Boyars, 1983) (*OC* III, 233–365)

The Absence of Myth: Writings on Surrealism, ed. Michael Richardson (London and New York: Verso, 1994)

'The Absence of Myth', in *The Absence of Myth*, 48 (*OC* XI, 236)

The Accursed Share [vol. I] (New York: Zone, 1991) (*OC* VII, 17–179)

The Accursed Share, vols II (*The History of Eroticism*) and III (*Sovereignty*) (New York: Zone, 1991) (*OC* VIII, 7–165 and 243–456 respectively)

'Architecture', in Leach (ed.), *Rethinking Architecture*, 21 (*OC* I, 171–2)

'Attraction and Repulsion I: Tropisms, Sexuality, Laughter and Tears', in Hollier

162 *Georges Bataille*

Guilty (Venice, CA: Lapis Press, 1988) (*OC* V, 235–392)

'Hegel, Death and Sacrifice', *Yale French Studies*, 78 (1990) (*OC* XII, 326–45)

The Impossible (San Francisco: City Lights, 1991) (*OC* III, 97–223)

Inner Experience (New York: SUNY Press, 1988) (*OC* V, 7–189)

'The Jésuve', in *Visions of Excess*, 73–8 (*OC* II, 13–20)

Literature and Evil (London: Calder and Boyars, 1973) (*OC* IX, 171–316)

'The Lugubrious Game', in *Visions of Excess*, 24–30 (*OC* I, 211–16)

Madame Edwarda see *My Mother . . .*

Manet (London: Macmillan, 1983) (*OC* IX, 103–67)

'Materialism', in *Visions of Excess*, 15–16 (*OC* I, 179–80)

'Museum', in Leach (ed.), *Rethinking Architecture*, 22–3 (*OC* I, 239–40)

My Mother/Madame Edwarda/The Dead Man (London: Marion Boyars, 1989) (*OC* IV, 175–276; *OC* III, 7–31; *OC* IV, 37–51)

'Nietzsche and the Fascists' in *Visions of Excess*, 182–96 (*OC* I, 447–65)

'Nietzschean Chronicle' in *Visions of Excess*, 202–12 (*OC* I, 477–90)

'The Notion of Expenditure', in *Visions of Excess*, 116–29 (*OC* I, 302–20)

'Notre Dame de Rheims', in Hollier (ed.), *Against Architecture*, 15–19 (*OC* I, 611–16)

'The Obelisk', in *Visions of Excess*, 213–22 (*OC* I, 501–13)

'The "Old Mole" and the Prefix *Sur* in the Words *Surhomme* and *Surrealist*', in *Visions of Excess*, 32–44 (*OC* II, 93–109)

On Nietzsche (London: Athlone, 1992) (*OC* VI, 7–205)

'The Pineal Eye', in *Visions of Excess*, 79–90 (*OC* II, 21–35)

'Popular Front in the Street', in *Visions of Excess*, 161–8 (*OC* I, 402–12)

'The Practice of Joy Before Death', in *Visions of Excess*, 235–9 (*OC* I, 552–8)

Prehistoric Painting: Lascaux or the Birth of Art (London: Macmillan, 1980) (*OC* IX, 7–101)

'The Psychological Structure of Fascism', in *Visions of Excess*, 137–60 (*OC* I, 339–71)

'The Sacred', in *Visions of Excess*, 240–5 (*OC* I, 559–63)

'Sacred Sociology and the Relationships between "Society", "Organism", and "Being"', in Hollier (ed.), *The College of Sociology*, 73–84 (*OC* II, 291–302)

'Sacrifices', in *Visions of Excess*, 130–6 (*OC* I, 89–96)

'Sacrificial Mutilation and the Severed Ear of Van Gogh', in *Visions of Excess*, 61–72 (*OC* I, 258– 70)

'Slaughterhouse', in Leach (ed.), *Rethinking Architecture*, 22 (*OC* I, 205)

'Solar Anus', in *Visions of Excess*, 5–9 (*OC* I, 79–86)

'The Sorcerer's Apprentice', in *Visions of Excess*, 223–34 (*OC* I, 523–37)

The Story of the Eye (London: Penguin, 1979) (*OC* I, 9–78)

'Take It or Leave It', in *The Absence of Myth*, 96 (*OC* XI, 130–1)

The Tears of Eros (San Francisco: City Lights, 1989) (*OC* X, 572–626)

Theory of Religion (New York: Zone, 1992) (*OC* VII, 281–361)

The Trial of Gilles de Rais (Los Angeles: Amok, 1991) (*OC* X, 271–571)

'The Use Value of D.A.F. de Sade (An Open Letter to My Current Comrades)', in *Visions of Excess*, 91–102 (*OC* II, 54–69)

Visions of Excess: Selected Writings, 1927–1939, ed. Allan Stoekl (Minneapolis: University of Minnesota Press, 1985)

Bataille: in French

L'Histoire de l'œil, *OC* I, 9–78
'L'anus solaire', *OC* I, 79–86
'Sacrifices', *OC* I, 89–96
'L'Amérique disparue', *OC* I, 152–8
'Architecture', *OC* I, 171–2
'Matérialisme', *OC* I, 179–80
'Œil', *OC* I, 187–9
'Abattoir', *OC* I, 205
'Le "Jeu lugubre"', *OC* I, 211–16
'Informe', *OC* I, 217
'Musée', *OC* I, 239–40
'L'art primitif', *OC* I, 247–54
'Joan Miró: peintures récentes', *OC* I, 255
'La mutilation sacrificielle et l'oreille coupée de Van Gogh', *OC* I, 258–70
'L'esprit moderne et le jeu des transpositions', *OC* I, 271–4
'La critique des fondements de la dialectique hégélienne', *OC* I, 277–90
'La notion de dépense', *OC* I, 302–20
'Le problème de l'État', *OC* I, 332–6
'La structure psychologique de fascisme', *OC* I, 339–71
'Contre-attaque: Union de Lutte des Intellectuels Révolutionnaires', *OC* I, 379–83
'Contre-attaque: appel à l'action', *OC* I, 395–7
'A ceux qui n'ont pas oublie la guerre du droit et de la liberte', *OC* I, 399–401
'Front Populaire dans la rue', *OC* I, 402–12
'Vers la révolution réelle', *OC* I, 413–28
'Nietzsche et les fascistes', *OC* I, 447–65
'Chronique nietzschéene', *OC* I, 477–90
'Van Gogh Prométhée, *OC* I, 497–500
'L'obélisque', *OC* I, 501–13
'L'apprenti sorcier', *OC* I, 523–37

'Sartre', *OC* XI, 226–8

'L'absence de mythe', *OC* XI, 236

'Lettre à Merleau-Ponty', *OC* XI, 251–2

'Réflexions sur le bourreau et le victime', *OC* XI, 262–7

'De l'existentialisme au primat de l'économie', *OC* XI, 279–306

'Le mensonge politique', *OC* XI, 332–8

'Nietzsche – William Blake', *OC* XI, 422–31

'Caprice et machinerie d'État à Stalingrad', *OC* XI, 472–9

'L'art, exercice de cruauté', *OC* XI, 480–6

'Molloy', *OC* XII, 85–94

'Silence et littérature', *OC* XII, 173–8

'La littérature française en 1952', *OC* XII, 237–40

'Hegel, la mort et le sacrifice', *OC* XII, 326–45

Choix de Lettres, 1917–1962 (Paris: Gallimard, 1997)

Works by Other Writers

Theodor Adorno, *Hegel: Three Studies* (Cambridge, MA: MIT Press, 1993)

Theodor Adorno, *Negating Dialectics* (London: Routledge and Kegan Paul 1973)

Alain Arnaud and Gisèle Excoffon-Lafarge, *Bataille* (Paris: Le Seuil, 1978)

Antonin Artaud, *The Theatre and its Double* (London: Calder, 1993)

Roland Barthes, 'The Metaphor of the Eye', in Bataille, *The Story of the Eye*, 119–27

Jean Baudrillard, *The Mirror of Production* (St Louis: Telos, 1975)

Jean Baudrillard, *Symbolic Exchange and Death* (London: Sage, 1993)

Jean Baudrillard, 'When Bataille Attacked the Metaphysical Principle of Economy', *Canadian Journal of Political and Social Theory*, 11 (3), (1987), 57–62

Walter Benjamin, 'The Work of Art in the Era of Mechanical Reproduction', in *Illuminations* (London: Fontana, 1973), 211–44

Geoff Bennington, 'Introduction to Economics I: Because the World Is Round', in

Judith Butler, *Gender Trouble: Feminism and the Subversion of Identity* (London: Routledge, 1989)

Roger Caillois, *L'Homme et le sacré*, third edition (Paris: Gallimard, 1950)

Cathy Caruth (ed.), *Trauma: Explorations in Memory* (Baltimore: John Hopkins University Press, 1995)

Hélène Cixous and Cathérine Clément, *The Newly Born Woman* (Manchester: Manchester University Press, 1986)

James Clifford, *The Predicament of Culture: Twentieth Century Ethnography, Literature and Art* (Cambridge, MA: Harvard University Press, 1988)

Simon Critchley, *Very Little, Almost Nothing: Death, Literature, Philosophy* (London: Routledge, 1997)

Gilles Deleuze, *Coldness and Cruelty*, in Deleuze/Sacher-Masoch, *Masochism* (New York: Zone, 1989)

Paul de Man, 'The Rhetoric of Blindness: Jacques Derrida's Reading of Rousseau', in *Blindness and Insight, Essays in the Rhetoric of Contemporary Criticism*, (Minneapolis: University of Minnesota Press, 1983), 102–41

Jacques Derrida, 'Economimesis', *Diacritics*, 11 (1981), 3–25

Jacques Derrida, *Ecriture et la différence* (Paris: Le Seuil, 1967)

Jacques Derrida, 'From Restricted to General Economy: A Hegelianism without Reserve', in *Writing and Difference* (London: Routledge, 1978), 251–77

Jacques Derrida, *Given Time I. Counterfeit Money* (Chicago: University of Chicago Press, 1992)

Jacques Derrida, *Of Grammatology* (Baltimore, MD and London: Johns Hopkins University Press, 1976)

Jacques Derrida, 'Parergon', in *The Truth in Painting* (Chicago and London: Chicago University Press, 1987), 15–147

Jacques Derrida, 'The Pit and the Pyramid: Introduction to Hegel's Semiology', in *Margins of Philosophy* (Chicago: University of Chicago Press, 1982), 69–108

Jacques Derrida, 'White Mythology', in *Margins of Philosophy* (Chicago: University of Chicago Press, 1982), 209–71

D.A.F. de Sade, *The 120 Days of Sodom* (London: Arrow, 1991)

Bernardinho de Sahagun, *General History of the Things of New Spain*, Book 2, *The Ceremonies* (Salt Lake City: University of Utah Press, 1982)

Georges Didi-Huberman, *La Ressemblance informe, ou le gai savoir visuel selon Georges Bataille* (Paris: Macula, 1995)

Mary Douglas, *Purity and Danger: An Analysis of the Concepts of Pollution and Taboo* (London: Routledge, 1991)

Emile Durkheim, *The Elementary Forms of Religious Life* (London: George Allen and Unwin, 1915)

Emile Durkheim, *The Rules of Sociological Method* (London: Macmillan, 1982)

Emile Durkheim and Marcel Mauss, *On Some Forms of Primitive Classification: Contribution to the Study of Collective Representations* (London: Cohen and West, 1969)

Andrea Dworkin, *Pornography: Men Possessing Women* (London: Women's Press, 1981)

Bret Easton Ellis, *American Psycho* (New York: Random House, 1991)

Friedrich Engels, *The Condition of the Working Class in England* (London: Penguin, 1987)

E.E. Evans-Pritchard, 'Introduction', in Mauss, *The Gift*, v–x

Hal Foster, *The Return of the Real* (Cambridge, MA and London: MIT Press, 1996)

Michel Foucault, *Discipline and Punish: The Birth of the Prison* (London: Penguin, 1991)

Michel Foucault, *The History of Sexuality*, vol. I (Harmondsworth: Penguin, 1990)

Michel Foucault, 'The Order of Discourse', in Robert Young (ed.), *Untying the Text: A Post-Structuralist Reader* (Boston and London: Routledge and Kegan Paul, 1981), 48–78

Michel Foucault, 'Preface to Transgression', in *Language, Counter-Memory and Practice* (New York: Cornell University Press, 1977), 29–52

Sigmund Freud, 'Beyond the Pleasure Principle', in *Standard Edition*, vol. XVIII (London: Hogarth Press, 1955), 7–64

Sigmund Freud, *Totem and Taboo* *Standard Edition*, vol. XIII (London: Hogarth Press, 1958), 1–162

Rodolphe Gasché, *The Tain of the Mirror: Derrida and the Philosophy of Reflection* (Cambridge, MA: Harvard University Press, 1986)

Carolyn Bailey Gill (ed.), *Bataille: Writing the Sacred* (London: Routledge, 1995)

René Girard, *The Scapegoat* (Baltimore, MD: Johns Hopkins University Press, 1989)

René Girard, *Violence and the Sacred* (Baltimore, MD: Johns Hopkins University Press, 1977)

Sue Golding, 'Solar Clitoris', *Parallax 4: Kojève's Paris/Now Bataille* (February 1997), 137–49

Clement Greenberg, *Art and Culture* (Boston: Beacon Press, 1961)

Elizabeth Grosz, *Volatile Bodies* (Sydney: Allen and Unwin, 1989)

Jürgen Habermas, 'The French Path to Postmodernity', *New German Critique*, 33 (Fall 1984), 79–102

G.W.F. Hegel, *Phenomenology of Spirit* (Oxford: Oxford University Press, 1977)

Martin Heidegger, *Being and Time* (Oxford: Blackwell, 1962)

Martin Heidegger, *Nietzsche, vol. IV, Nihilism* (San Francisco, Harper and Row,

Aileen Kelly, *Mikhail Bakunin: A Study in the Psychology and Politics of Utopianism* (New Haven and London: Yale University Press, 1987)

Pierre Klossowski, *Sade My Neighbour* (London: Quartet, 1992)

Sarah Kofman, *Nietzsche and Metaphor* (London: Athlone, 1993)

Alexandre Kojève, *Introduction à la lecture de Hegel* (Paris: Gallimard, 1947)

Alexandre Kojève, *Introduction to the Reading of Hegel* (New York: Basic Books, 1969)

Rosalind Krauss and Yves-Alain Bois, *Formless: A User's Guide* (New York: Zone, 1997)

Julia Kristeva, *Powers of Horror: An Essay on Abjection* (New York: Columbia University Press, 1982)

Julia Kristeva, *Tales of Love* (New York: Columbia University Press, 1987)

Nick Land, *The Thirst for Annihilation: Georges Bataille and Virulent Nihilism* (London: Routledge, 1992)

Laure (Colette Peignot), *Laure: The Collected Writings* (San Francisco: City Lights, 1995)

Neil Leach (ed.), *Rethinking Architecture* (London: Routledge, 1997)

Annie Leclerc, *Parole de femme*, extract in Toril Moi (ed.), *French Feminist Thought: A Reader* (Cambridge, MA and Oxford: Blackwell, 1987), 73–9

Claude Lévi-Strauss, 'Introduction à l'œuvre de Marcel Mauss', in M. Mauss, *Sociologie et anthropologie* (Paris: PUF, 1985), ix–lii

Francis Marmande, *Georges Bataille politique* (Lyon: Presses Universitaires de Lyon, 1985)

Marcel Mauss, *The Gift: Forms and Functions of Exchange in Archaic Societies* (London: Routledge and Kegan Paul, 1966)

Marcel Mauss, *Sociologie et anthropologie* (Paris: PUF, 1985), ix–lii

Arne Naess, *Ecology, Community and Lifestyle* (Cambridge: Cambridge University Press, 1989)

Jean-Luc Nancy, *The Inoperative Community* (Minneapolis: University of Minnesota Press, 1991)

Friedrich Nietzsche, *The Twilight of the Idols* and *The Antichrist* (Harmondsworth: Penguin, 1989)

Friedrich Nietzsche, *On The Genealogy of Morals* and *Ecce Homo* (New York: Vintage, 1968)

Friedrich Nietzsche, *Thus Spake Zarathustra* (Harmondsworth: Penguin, 1961)

Julian Pefanis, *Heterology and the Postmodern: Bataille, Baudrillard and Lyotard* (Durham, NC and London: Duke University Press, 1991)

Pauline Réage, *The Story of O* (London: Corgi, 1994)

Michael Richardson, *Georges Bataille* (London: Routledge, 1994)

Michèle Richman, *Reading Georges Bataille: Beyond the Gift* (Baltimore, MD: Johns Hopkins University Press, 1982)

Gillian Rose, *Mourning Becomes the Law* (Cambridge: Cambridge University Press, 1996)

Jean-Jacques Rousseau, *The Social Contract and Discourses* (London: Dent, 1913)

Marshall Sahlins, *Stone Age Economics* (London: Tavistock, 1974)

Jean-Paul Sartre, *Being and Nothingness: An Essay on Phenomenological Ontology* (London: Methuen, 1972)

Jean-Paul Sartre, 'Un nouveau mystique', in *Situations I* (Paris: Gallimard, 1947), 143–88

Jean-Paul Sartre, *Saint Genet: comédien et martyr* (Paris: Gallimard, 1952)

Phillipe Sollers, *L'Écriture et l'expérience des limites* (Paris: Le Seuil, 1968)

Susan Sontag, 'The Pornographic Imagination', in Bataille, *The Story of the Eye*, 83–118

Judith Still, *Feminine Economies: Thinking against the Market in the Enlightenment and the Late Twentieth Century* (Manchester: Manchester University Press, 1997)

Judith Still, 'Horror in Kristeva and Bataille', *Paragraph*, 20 (1997), 221–39

Susan Rubin Suleiman, 'Pornography, Transgression and the Avant-Garde: Bataille's *Story of the Eye*', in Nancy K. Miller (ed.), *The Poetics of Gender* (New York: Columbia University Press, 1986), 117–36

Michel Surya, *Georges Bataille: la mort à l'œuvre* (Paris: Gallimard, 1992)

Tzvetan Todorov, *The Conquest of America* (New York: Harper and Row, 1984)

Index